ANCIENT WISDOM
PRESENT DAY HEALING

Ancient Wisdom
Present Day Healing

Here am I, here are you:
But what does it mean?
What are we going to do?

W.H. Auden

Barrie Anson
DHoM, MRadA, DHD, PsyV

Published in the UK 1999

Copyright Barrie Anson 1999

Cover photograph by Michael MacGregor
Cover layout by Trudy Leer
Chapter illustration by Lisa Dickinson

Published by Lumiere Publications
Naboth Vineyard
Newtown
Minstead SO43 7GD
email: lumiere99@hotmail.com
ISBN 0 9535654 0 8

Printed and bound by The Baskerville Press Ltd.
Salisbury Wiltshire

For Stuart & family

CONTENTS

FOREWORD
by Dr Ronald Livingston MBBS London, MFHom.

Having practised homoeopathic medicine for more than half a century I welcome the publication of this God inspired, uplifting book. Holistic medicine, such as homoeopathy, provides an opportunity to blend medicine with spirituality and Barrie Anson's outstanding work details the significance of the latter. He gives very readable descriptions of what I might describe as 'spiritual medicine' and suggests ways in which we can heal both ourselves and others.

Death is a taboo subject in this day and age - people have always feared it, or rather, the unknown. In the modern world the two professions of doctor and priest have been sharply segregated. The doctor treats his patient's body but stops short of discussing spiritual matters, especially death, which tends to be regarded as a medical failure. The priest may, eventually, be summoned but, probably rather late in the day! Barrie Anson suggests that the Ancient Wisdom teachings, which are to be found in the scriptures of all religions and in the collective unconscious of the human race, offer great comfort to us all. He gently explains that it is impossible to die and that so called death is simply a change of state - something to be welcomed rather than feared.

Profound subjects are touched upon in a simple and straightforward way and the reader is left with a magically increased awareness of the love, or light, in himself, in his fellow men and women, the light in all that lives and moves and, indeed, in the earth itself.

All creation responds to love - world literature, especially poetry, music, painting, sculpture and dance testify to this. Only if love is permitted to play its part in human nature can we experience a full and satisfying occupation on our planet. Without it something essential is lost. Love never dies - it is an indivisible and eternal universal jewel to enjoy and to use - both in giving and receiving.

This book is uplifting, lucid, simple and a pleasure to read. It will be welcomed by seekers and sufferers alike - that is by all of us.

ABOUT THE AUTHOR

Barrie Anson was born in 1938, brought up in the New Forest area and educated at Brockenhurst School.

After school he entered the commercial world in London. This era came to an abrupt end in March 1957 with the commencement of two years compulsory National service in the Army. About half of this time was spent training in Yorkshire and the remainder in Hong Kong. It was clear, at an early stage, that he had little aptitude for the military life and having completed the required 728 days (which he counted) he began a marketing career in the pharmaceutical industry.

Initially based in London his career continued in the Far East where he was based in Bangkok. After some years in Thailand as Marketing Manager for an American drug manufacturer he was later posted to Lagos, Nigeria. Following a personal crisis he opted out of big business to live in Athens, Greece. After a series of adventures there and much international travel he lived briefly in France where his interest in spiritual matters began to emerge.

Returning to England in the late 1970's, the author worked in the health food trade, later training in homoeopathy, radionics, nutritional therapy and hypnotherapy. He has been in practice in Hampshire and Dorset since 1979.

ACKNOWLEDGEMENTS

I would like to acknowledge the help and inspiration I have obtained from the many volumes published by the White Eagle Publishing Trust, Liss, Hampshire. I would also like to thank the various friends whose comments have helped in the preparation of this book. In particular Hilary Brenan deserves praise for her patience in revealing the intricacies of word processing; Joan Portbury for her textual corrections and helpful observations and Peter Nevile for his encouragement to get the book published. I am very grateful to them all. Finally I am indebted to the following publishers for permission to quote from the books listed below:

ON THE DEATH OF MY SON by Jasper Swain. The Aquarian Press, now Harper Collins Publishers, 77-85 Fulham Palace Road, Hammersmith, London

TRUTH IS VEILED by Peter Cowlin. Synthesis Publishing, Portelet, Binstead Hall, Binstead, Isle of Wight. Distributed by Michael Cowlin Tel. 01491 872985.

PRIVATE DOWDING by Wellesley Tudor Pole. Pilgrims Book Services, Tasburgh, Norwich.

THE AWAKENING LETTERS compiled by Rosamond Lehmann and Cynthia Sandys. Neville Spearman Ltd., Saffron Walden, Essex.

THE GOLDEN KEY by Percy Welsford. Psychic Press Ltd., 2 Tavistock Chambers, Bloomsbury Way, London WC1A 2SE. Tel. 071 405 3340.

A CREED by John Masefield

I hold that when a person dies
His soul returns again to earth;
Arrayed in some new flesh disguise,
Another mother gives him birth,
With sturdier limbs and brighter brain
The old soul takes the roads again.

Such is my belief and trust;
This hand, this hand that holds the pen
Has many a hundred times been dust
And turned to dust again;
These eyes of mine have blinked and shone
In Thebes, in Troy, in Babylon.

All that I rightly think or do,
Or make or spoil, or bless or blast,
Is curse or blessing justly due
For sloth or effort in the past.
My life's a statement of the sum
Of vice indulged, or overcome.

And as I wander on the roads
I shall be helped and healed and blessed;
Kind words shall cheer and be as goads
To urge to heights before unguessed.
My road shall be the road I made,
All that I gave shall be repaid.

So shall I fight, so shall I tread,
In this long war beneath the stars;
So shall a glory wreathe my head;
So shall I faint and show the scars,
Until this case, this clogging mould,
Be smithied all to kingly gold.

Introduction

All things by immortal power, near or far,
Hiddenly to each other, linked are;
That thou can'st not stir a flower,
Without the troubling of a star.
Francis Thompson

The above few lines by Francis Thompson say a great deal. If everybody appreciated the fundamental truth contained in these words and realised how inter-connected we all are - that is everybody and everything, they would surely treat one another differently. Why, for example, would one fight a war with a part of oneself? We all emanate from the same source and remain part of the whole. All creation is one.

As a homoeopath and natural medicine practitioner I find that there is an area which has been neglected in regard to health and well-being. It is that optimistic philosophy and understanding that takes into account the meaning of life and what happens when our life on Earth finishes. This book is an endeavour to give some hope and encouragement for those who have a fear of death and who have avoided any consideration of this and the wider implications of their *dis-ease* or lack of harmony.

Since life is eternal and we are all on a long journey I believe that it is worth giving some thought to our reasons for being here. We are all on the same voyage and, whilst our routes might be a little different, we are heading in the same direction. There are so many unanswered questions about the mystery of life and death but I hope what follows will help to answer some of them. By addressing such issues now I trust that fellow travellers on the journey through life will find their path easier.

My own experience, like that of most people I know, has often been painful but we are all here to learn and usually need uncomfortable events to bring lessons home to us. Fortunately, as we learn to be kinder to ourselves and others we find that life becomes easier. Experience teaches us that we reap as we sow. We also begin to understand that we need to love one another.

The main content of this book was originally published as three separate volumes called HOLISM, HOMOEOPATHY, HEAL-ING and the HEREAFTER, LOVE ONE ANOTHER and SEEING THE LIGHT. In combining the three volumes I have taken out a few items and added some others.

In the original research I learned a great deal using a variety of sources. However all the information is taken from published material widely available to anybody. The book starts with a comparison of orthodox and holistic therapy and touches on the importance of breathing properly. Nutritional therapy, homoe-opathy, hypnotherapy and healing are discussed as these form part of my own practice. The book continues with some suggestions about our reasons for being on the planet, spiritu-ality versus religion, some notes about the work of the *great teachers* of the world and what is collectively known as the *ancient wisdom.*

The subjects of clairvoyance, subtle bodies, reincarnation and karma are discussed and associated items. After that there are some thoughts about what happens when we move on from this earthly life. In the chapters that follow there are extracts from various sources revealing personal experiences of life after accidental death. Inevitably, the latter is *channelled* informa-tion and, whilst I am aware that not everybody can accept such sources, I urge the reader to consider them with an open mind. The book concludes with some suggestions about how we might progress spiritually and how to incorporate that into our daily lives.

These are challenging times and most of us need all the help we can get. Sometimes it is easy to forget that we should be grateful for the opportunity of living now and that the challenges that come our way are opportunities for spiritual growth. There are moments when the lives of others seem so much easier than our own but this is probably an illusion! On our road to initiation we need to overcome the daily obstacles with courage and determination. I hope this book will help to remove the fear of death and help people to love one another. In my view love, unconditional love that is, and spirituality go hand in hand.

I use the word man in this book to mean both man and woman and refer to the Creator as He although it is my understanding that the Parent-of-All is both male and female. I trust I will be forgiven by anybody who feels strongly about such issues. It is not my intention to offend the belief of any individual but if, inadvertently, I do so in the course of this book then I apologise whole-heartedly.

Barrie Anson, Brockenhurst 1998

1

Orthodox or Conventional Medicine Compared with Holistic Therapy

*Science is a splendid piece of furniture to have on the first floor,
as long as there is good sense on the ground floor.*
W. Holmes

There is a great difference in the approach to healing in the two
systems. The holistic (whole-istic) approach is gentler and
treats the patient at every level which is to say mentally,
emotionally and physically. Orthodox or conventional medicine, in general terms, is concerned with treating symptoms and
has been likened to a plumber finding a leak and plugging it
rather than reviewing the whole system.

It is an unfortunate fact of life that most orthodox general
practitioners have a hefty work load and, as a consequence, they
are not always able to devote time to listening to their patient's
problems. On the other hand, the holistic practitioner is quite
often able to help a patient simply by allowing sufficient time
to do this.

To understand the gentler or holistic approach one must first know a little about conventional medicine, sometimes known as allopathy because it uses allopathic medicines (more about this later). Whilst two centuries ago conventional medicine was a blend of crude science, myth and superstition, today it is overwhelmingly scientific. It is so scientific and specialised that the individual with a serious health problem is quite likely to be put in the hands of a specialist. The expertise of a specialist is usually concentrated in dealing with just one aspect of illness and sometimes this makes it difficult for the whole picture to be seen - an inability to see the *wood* for the *trees*. By contrast the holistic approach, which involves getting an overall picture of the *wood*, can frequently identify the real cause of the disease.

There is a point of view which says that modern medicine, as we know it, has done little to cure or prevent disease when compared with the advantages conferred on society by good sanitation, improved housing, smaller families and other social improvements. It is true to say that a handful of drug innovations, such as antibiotics, have made a difference to life expectancy. However, I suspect it is wrong to believe that these innovations are responsible for saving the many millions of lives that one might imagine. It is well known that many killer infectious diseases were fast disappearing before drugs were available to cure them. Even tuberculosis was eradicated much more by social conditions than by drugs. The problem now is disease brought about by the over-use of drugs and antibiotics.

In general terms orthodox medicine tends to see every new case, especially of chronic disease, as a chance event. If a person develops cancer or gallstones or has some obscure disease then it is usually considered to be bad luck. The connection with what has gone before is often ignored. In an individual you might see a condition that manifested 10 years ago which we can call (a). 5 years later the same individual appears in front of his doctor with another condition - let's call it (b). When he appears in front of his doctor today with condition (c) it is unlikely that the doctor will be aware of the thread connecting those 3 conditions. Probably it was the suppression of condition (a) which led to the foundation of (b) and the suppression of (b) which later resulted in condition (c).

An example of the connection between various conditions might be that of a child fed with cow's milk. This can result in poor gut flora and possibly a zinc deficiency. Because of the poor gut flora and inability to deal with dairy products catarrh might result. In later years poor gut flora might cause constipation and a build-up of toxins. Tonsillitis could develop and this would likely be treated with antibiotics. If that proved unhelpful the tonsils might then have been removed. That action might have resolved the immediate problem but in the long term would probably make the situation worse. Later in life appendicitis might develop and the appendix removed as a consequence. In the following years one might expect irritable bowel syndrome, with its attendant problems and, eventually arthritis might appear or, worse still, cancer.

Drugs and surgery are both suppressive treatments. Suppression equals a reduction of the vital force (or life force as it is sometimes called). This results in disease becoming chronic because the body is unable to throw off the toxic overload. A famous naturopath called Dr Lindlahr said that .... *every acute disease is the result of a cleansing and healing effort on the part of nature...*

When nature tries to show her hand by giving us a cold or a fever most people reach for an aspirin and immediately suppress this healing attempt. This is the orthodox way of doing things.

Some years ago I came across a story that illustrates disease suppression in a dramatic way. It was entitled WE DID OUR BEST and it goes like this:

A young man developed a sore throat. He went to his physician who prescribed penicillin for the inflammation. The sore throat promptly disappeared. Three days later he developed itching and hives all over his body. A doctor correctly diagnosed a penicillin reaction and prescribed anti-histamines. The hives went away!

However, the anti-histamines caused the patient to be drowsy and he cut his hand whilst at work. He went to the company nurse who put some anti-bacterial salve on the injury. Unhappily, the salve contained penicillin which caused the hives to return. Recognising a possible serious reaction to penicillin for the second time his doctor then prescribed cortisone. The hives disappeared once more.

The patient then developed abdominal pains and noticed blood in his stools. The correct diagnosis was made of a bleeding peptic ulcer brought on by the cortisone. Sadly, as the patient failed to respond to standard measures to correct the haemorrhage, the next course of action indicated was a partial gastrectomy (removal of part of the stomach). Fortunately the surgery was successful - the stomach pains diminished and the bleeding stopped but as the patient had previously lost so much blood due to haemorrhaging and during surgery a blood transfusion was needed. He was given 2 pints of blood.

Unfortunately he contracted hepatitis from the transfusion but, thanks to being young and vital, he recovered from the hepatitis.

Unhappily, at the point of insertion of the transfusion needle, a painful red swelling appeared which indicated a probable infection. Having had previous bad experience with penicillin the drug of choice was now tetracycline. This was given and the infection promptly subsided.

Disruption of the intestinal flora by the tetracycline caused painful abdominal spasms and severe diarrhoea. As a result the patient was now given an anti-spasmodic drug. This medicine was in the belladonna, or muscle relaxant, group of drugs which relaxed the smooth muscles all over his body. The effect of the muscle relaxant on the eye muscles of the patient impaired his vision...... he drove his car into a tree and was killed instantly!

This is reputed to be true story and, if it isn't, it certainly could be - it shows that the use of modern drugs and surgery is not always the answer despite the very best of intentions. The medical establishment has little time for unorthodoxy although, it has to be said, times are changing and it is encouraging to note that a number of conventional doctors are now showing some interest in holistic therapies.

Some of my natural medicine colleagues are much opposed to orthodoxy but my personal belief is that conventional medicine cannot be dismissed so easily. The gentle approach does not have all the answers. I know that if I get run over I shall be only too pleased to receive orthodox treatment including surgery. In the area of surgery and microsurgery there have been brilliant achievements. I am personally not in favour of transferring a heart from one person to another but it is a difficult line to draw. Some of the orthodox technical *know-how* is very valuable and we must take account of the diagnostic procedures available to it. In my view the two approaches must be blended, where appropriate, for the benefit of those who are unwell.

2

LIVING TO EAT OR EATING TO LIVE

Let food be your medicine and medicine be your food.
Hippocrates

Nutritional therapy is a form of complementary medicine in which the practitioner works with a patient to help them improve their diet and understanding of how their body functions. By ridding the body of exposure to substances which are stressful to it and by improving the assimilation of those foods which are useful it is possible to make significant improvements to health and well-being. An efficiently functioning body finds it easier to repair and heal itself.

The entire human body is made from food plus air and water. This simple but profound statement means that the quality of food we eat is very important to our health. However, the area of nutrition is one which has been more or less ignored in conventional medicine until relatively recently. We are advised to eat a balanced diet - whatever that might mean! At the time of writing it does seem that the government is at last turning its attention to the importance of diet and preventive medicine so perhaps we should not be too discouraged. I cannot resist the

17

opportunity of expressing my view that a wholefood diet, rich in vegetables and with a minimum of animal foods and especially animal fats, is much better than one full of refined sugar products, processed foods and parts of animals.

As already stated the food we eat is very important. We are what we eat or rather what we absorb. There is an interesting book about diet and delinquency by Dr Alexander Schauss. The thrust of it is that many criminals are not born bad but simply commit crimes because they feel bad. The reason they feel so bad is because they eat so badly. To cut a long story short they eat quantities of junk food, overloaded with sugar and additives of one sort or another with the result that they are frequently nutritionally deficient or simply suffering with hypoglycaemia (low blood sugar). Such mineral deficiencies and abnormal blood sugar levels can influence mood and cause all kinds of aberrant behaviour.

Organically grown foods have a greater *vitality*, or *life force*, than fruits or vegetables conventionally produced using artificial fertilisers, pesticides, etc. According to some tests, which measured units of light emitted from organic and conventionally grown food, organically grown food gave consistently higher *readings* than that grown conventionally. This light energy is thought to be stored in the DNA during photosynthesis when plants are busy converting sunlight and water to organic material. The light is transmitted continuously by every cell. The theory is that the higher the level of light energy a cell emits then the greater is it's vitality. Thus there is more potential for the transfer of that energy to someone eating the food. In short, for increased life force, or vitality, it helps to eat organically grown foods.

In my experience there are some commonly used foods which many of my patients have eliminated or minimised in their diets with remarkable benefits. These are milk, milk based products, wheat and wheat based products. Refined sugar and salt are also to be discouraged.

According to some nutritionists one of the prime problems with milk is that it makes for poor intestinal absorption because it neutralises stomach acid, leaving protein only partly digested. Milk forms an excessive and unhealthy mucous in the digestive tract which, combined with other food residues, hardens to inhibit the absorption of minerals and other nutrients. Milk encourages alkali forming putrefactive bacteria to live in the intestines, again creating conditions unsuitable for mineral absorption. The high calcium content of milk itself is frequently not absorbed for this reason.

It is worth bearing in mind that cows discourage their calves from consuming milk after weaning. In short, cow's milk is good for young calves as human milk is good for young babies. Once beyond babyhood milk is not a useful food - especially cow's milk for humans! In cow's milk, casein, the main protein, is poorly digested by humans and, additionally, it may contain hormones secreted by the cow's pituitary gland, including growth hormone which is not destroyed by processing. Such milk can lead to unnatural growth in children.

The mucus forming tendency of milk in connection with the intestines applies equally to the mucus membranes of the nose, sinuses, etc., causing catarrh, hay fever, fallopian tube blockages, Eustachian tube blockages and so on. Remember that cheese is concentrated milk and has a high salt content.
Milk encourages sodium (salt) to enter the cells and the eventual

result of this is energy depletion. A sodium excess in the diet over a long period overwhelms the mechanism in the body to deal with this excess and results in a rise in acidity and sodium concentration. The two tend to go hand in hand. The mineral magnesium gets excluded from the cells and as a consequence the sodium pump mechanism can no longer work efficiently. The resulting intracellular magnesium deficiency exacerbates the situation still further and a vicious cycle is created. Potassium is also lost from the cells under these circumstances and trace elements such as zinc, manganese and chromium tend to be denied access to the cells.

A lot of different minerals are critical to the mechanism which controls blood sugar levels. Calcium metabolism is also severely affected and blood sugar levels are very closely related to the blood calcium level. If there is a drop in the blood sugar level, because of a drop in the blood calcium level, the individual will suffer a loss of energy. The normal body response would be for the pancreas and adrenal glands to go into action but if there is a lack of trace minerals in the body they will have difficulty in doing so and pancreatic and adrenal exhaustion may eventually result.

Sugary foods such as cakes, chocolate bars, sweets, biscuits, pastries, etc. and stimulant beverages such as tea, coffee, *coke,* etc. cause the blood sugar to rise initially (hence the craving for them) but then the level falls quickly and causes severe mineral loss. Another vicious cycle begins and progressively stronger stimulants are needed to pick-up the individual lacking energy. Sometimes, when the blood sugar level drops very low, odd patterns of behaviour can occur such as bursts of temper, tearfulness and so on. Conditions including the pre-menstrual syndrome, migraine, asthma, epilepsy, colitis and irritable bowel syndrome may be provoked or become more severe at these times.

A sluggish intestine is one of the results of eating gluten containing foods, especially wheat products such as bread, pasta and pastries. It is due to the glue-like quality it assumes when poorly digested and mixed with mucus and other liquids in the digestive tract. The gluey substance adheres to and lines the walls of the colon making for poor absorption. Peristaltic movement (which normally moves the content of the intestine) is less effective and the sluggishness builds on itself. Putrefying bacteria invading this almost stationary mass contributes towards auto-intoxication. Diverticuli (pockets in the bowel) may develop thus exacerbating the situation by providing a home for more bacteria and toxins with direct access into the bloodstream.

I realise that avoiding wheat and dairy products is not very easy but the rewards are considerable. If one cannot avoid them totally then it is worth minimising the intake of these items as well as refined sugar products and salt.

3

VEGETARIAN - TO BE OR NOT TO BE?

I have no doubt that it is a part of the destiny of the human race,
in its gradual improvement, to leave off eating animals, as surely
as the savage tribes have left off eating each other when they
come in contact with the more civilised.
Thoreau

There are many discussions about what is natural for humans to
eat. If one looks at the diet of mammals there are two groups
- flesh-eating animals such as dogs, cats, tigers and lions and
vegetarian animals like cows, bulls, horses, camels, giraffes and
even the mighty elephants.

When comparing their physical features the flesh-eating animals
have long teeth to tear the raw animal flesh from the bones
whilst the other animals have flat teeth for grinding vegetable
food. Meat-eating animals have rough tongues to lick flesh
from the bone and sharp strong claws to catch and kill their prey
unlike the vegetarian creatures. Interestingly, too, they have
excellent night vision for hunting whilst the vegetarians have
more difficulty in seeing after dusk.

Less obvious are differences in the intestines. In the meat-eating group these are generally only 2 to 3 times the body length thus facilitating the rapid passage of the meat eaten before it has time to putrefy. In vegetarian animals the intestines are generally 6 to 7 times the length of their bodies because the contents need to be retained for a longer period. Vegetarian creatures have digestive enzymes in their saliva and begin digesting food whilst it is still in the mouth. They also have a different pH in both their stomachs and saliva than the flesh-eating creatures. By the way pH is a measure of acidity or alkalinity where pH7 is neutral. Below pH7 acidity increases and above it alkalinity increases and starch digestion is thought to require alkaline conditions whereas protein digestion, for example meat, requires acid conditions.

Humans have flat teeth for grinding like the vegetarian animals and smoother tongues than the carnivores who tend to gulp their food without much chewing. Humans are (usually) without sharp claws and their vision is not very good after dusk. Generally speaking human intestines are about 26 feet long or 6 to 7 times as long as the trunks of their bodies. The pH of human saliva is similar to vegetarian animals and, like them, the saliva contains digestive enzymes. In these respects of physical design humans certainly have a lot in common with the non meat-eating animals.

If one looks carefully at the differences in behaviour between meat-eating and vegetarian animals at a zoo it will be observed that the meat eaters can be fierce and aggressive. The cages of the meat-eaters will smell strongly in line with everything that exudes from their bodies. On the other hand the vegetarian animals are relatively calm and gentle.

When an animal is killed its body immediately starts to decay. Anybody eating meat is literally eating dead matter. This rapid decaying process is one reason why animal matter leaves so much toxic material in the systems of those consuming it.

Vegetables may dehydrate after they are chopped but it will take quite some time for those vegetables to decay.

Some people argue that it is possible to find animals to eat that are healthy and this is true to some extent but, in the factory production and killing systems prevalent nowadays, all kinds of undesirable toxins and hormones permeate the body tissues at the moment of slaughter. Those residues remain in the meat which is later consumed. Because human intestines are so long the decayed flesh cannot be digested and pass through the body before putrefying. The body tries to filter out toxins through the eliminative system, including perspiration and breath, and it is this process which can cause foul perspiration odour. Those remaining will contribute to the overall toxic load in the body which is the precursor of disease.

Carnivorous humans correctly point out that meat is a rich source of protein. However, it is known that humans do not need such a concentrated protein to metabolise the body. Vegetarians believe that protein should be as close to its natural source as possible. It is plentiful, in simpler chemical form and thus easier to digest, in soya beans, lentils, avocados, nuts and in seeds such as pumpkin and sunflower. In any event the need for large amounts of protein is much exaggerated in the West and the problem here is often one of excess rather than insufficiency.

Vegetarians claim to have bodies that are healthier, more supple and less tense than those of their animal eating counterparts.

Various studies have shown the benefits of vegetarianism. They have indicated very positive effects but for some people more scientific evidence is required. Perhaps trials on a grand scale, at some point in the future, will provide the kind of evidence that is needed?

It would probably be difficult to convince an Eskimo whose diet is primarily meat that he should be vegetarian because he would starve without it. Clearly a vegetarian diet in such an environment, where even grass does not grow, would be impossible. It is interesting to note that the average life span of an Eskimo is quite short. The Hunzas of Pakistan whose diet is primarily vegetarian live very long lives with recorded ages of 110 years not uncommon. People who eat a lot of meat are often concerned that they will be unable to keep up their strength without it but horses, oxen, bulls and elephants do not seem to have a problem!

The violence in our society poses a threat to its very existence. There are those who believe that the meat diet is part of that violence. It involves killing, often in hideous circumstances and on a grand scale. Most people who have witnessed how animals die in a slaughter house cannot help but be influenced by it. However there is a curious double standard in that many people who would be unable to carry out or even witness such events are happy to allow other people to do it on their behalf. Equally many pet lovers will go to great lengths to prevent cruelty to some animals but at the same time encourage a trade which brings about the deaths of countless lambs, calves and cows. One wonders about the difference between a cow's life and that of a cat? Perhaps the cow is missing a pet name? In some oriental countries dogs and cats are considered delicacies for human consumption

There are many who believe that there will always be wars so long as man continues to treat animals inhumanely. When we eat vegetables we are also destroying something but we have to eat and the plant is not as developed as the animal in the expression of its consciousness. Vegetables have not achieved individual consciousness. The more developed the expression of that consciousness in a particular form of life the more pain is felt when it is destroyed.

Cutting off the branch of a tree causes less pain than cutting of the limb of an animal. Studies have shown that plants do experience pain but it is not considered to be on the same level as that experienced by warm-blooded creatures with a developed nervous system. The Hindu scriptures talk about ...*consciousness sleeping in the mineral kingdom, dreaming in plant life and awakening in animal life...* It is a similar consciousness in all but functioning at different levels. For instance in animals we see instinct functioning and in humans there is intelligence.

There are other considerations also and two of these are the economic and ecological ones. There is certainly an unequal distribution of food in the world and the starvation experienced in some parts is sometimes blamed on overpopulation there. There is another point of view however which is that the resources we have are adequate if we are willing to share them equally. According to some sources it needs 16 pounds of grain to be fed to a bull in order to get 1lb of meat. This amount of grain would go a lot further if fed directly to humans. Looked at another way an acre of land used for grain production gives 5 times as much protein as an acre used for producing meat. An acre of beans or lentils gives 10 times as much protein and an acre of vegetables 15 times as much protein.

As mentioned above meat is a rich source of minerals and the smell of meat cooking is very appetising for many people. It has to be borne in mind that the meat industry would be doomed without the present demand for it. These are considerations to be borne in mind when weighing the arguments and it is for individuals to decide where their priorities lie.

For those who do wish to stop eating meat I believe that the transition should be made gradually. Initially one could start by avoiding red meat whilst continuing to eat fowl and fish for some time. Later fowl can be left out of the diet, leaving fish and eggs and eventually graduating to vegetarian food only. A body which is used to eating flesh may still demand it, in the same way that the body of a smoker who has relinquished the habit, craves nicotine. The cells remember it so there may be some difficulty at first. However as the body becomes less toxic it will become easier.

Whatever we decide to eat it is as well to do so with a feeling of gratitude and to bear in mind the words of Mahatma Gandhi who said...*the earth has enough for everyone's need but not enough for everyone's greed.*

4

A WORD ON BREATHING

Basically all healing is the intake into the body of the eternal sun,
the light. We need to call upon this light, breathe it in, see it and
live consciously in it.
White Eagle

Since breathing is central to all the functions of the body it is
important that we understand how to breathe deeply. Proper
breathing is much neglected and overlooked and yet has a
profound effect on health. It can enhance vitality and well-
being and also bring tranquillity and harmony into our lives.
Breathing influences us physically, emotionally and mentally.
The breath is a marvellous tool not only for helping us to relax
but also to make us more aware.

Many people spend their entire lives using only a small part of
their lungs. When this is the case there will always be a residue
of stale air left inside. In some instances this could become toxic
with consequent ill effects throughout the system. If you would
like to improve your general breathing here is a technique you
may like to try:

Start by sitting comfortably on a firm chair in a relaxed fashion but keep the spine straight. Some people may prefer to lie flat on the floor instead of sitting. In the latter case a folded blanket or a rug beneath the body is helpful to ensure comfort and relaxation. An extra folded blanket under the top half of the body from waist to head facilitates expansion of the chest and helps the free flow of air.

Close your eyes and inwardly observe the breath flowing in and out for a few minutes. Connect to this rhythm and sense the breath becoming softer, deeper and slower. After a while become aware of the phases of the breath:

How the inhalation starts at the base of the lungs with the gentle movement of the diaphragm.

How it then moves to the middle of the lungs as the rib cage rises upwards and outwards.

And, finally how the breath rises to the very top of the lungs with a quiet smooth movement. The upper ribs slide under the collar bones and sideways towards the armpits.

The exhalation follows the same pattern in the reverse order, starting at the base and working upwards as the breath quietly leaves the body Please note the comments below about extending the exhalation when you wish to promote relaxation.

Breathing in this deep, conscious manner should never be forced but done with quiet concentration. As you continue the breath will naturally deepen and the lung capacity will expand.

After a few minutes of being aware of these movements visualise the breath as light. On the inward breath take the light

to the heart centre (the area around the centre of the chest). On
the outward breath see the light as rays of the sun radiating to
every part of your body and filling every cell with light.

If you practise this you will become aware of the form and shape of your body as light. Ten minutes a day of quiet concentration on the art of breathing will bring enormous benefits. It may encourage a deeper study of the connection between the breath and the more subtle levels of our being.

So far as relaxation is concerned it is helpful to extend the exhalation of the breath for as long as it is comfortable. Rhythmic breathing, with long slow out-breaths, followed by a short pause really winds down the busy brain-waves from the active beta state to the clearer and more centred alpha state. In life we tend to cling on to situations, people, thoughts and ideas and, as a consequence, we tend to hang on to our breath as well. Lengthening the out-breath will facilitate letting go of stress and tension and help to antidote high blood pressure. It can also help us to let go of physical and mental clutter.

It is worth noting that in stressful situations breathing is likely to become shallow and consequently oxygen is taken only to the upper part of the lungs. The tendency is to hold on to the solar plexus area thus restricting the movement of the diaphragm and, in turn, inhibiting the action of our lungs. Try to observe yourself when you are next feeling anxious and remember that this is the moment to relax the abdomen consciously, breathing-out slowly and completely. If you do this the in-breath will take care of itself. Practising the sort of breathing will promote relaxation and remove anxiety. When you are ready to go back to full activity, for example after meditation, just reverse the procedure by deepening the in-breath, holding on to that air for a few moments, then gradually shortening the out-breath until balance is achieved again.

At another level the conscious breathing-in of the light and conscious breathing-out of love to mankind is immensely valuable. This deep rhythmic breathing does more than affect the body. Seen clairvoyantly, the person breathing in the light and being aware of this divine breath is strengthening his soul and causing it to radiate a great light. Such light is able to traverse the world and, indeed, the universe.

5

HOMOEOPATHY

Science has the first word on everything and the last word on nothing.
Victor Hugo

Homoeopathy is just one of the many holistic approaches to disease. To many people it presents a baffling and unscientific collection of contradictions because it uses poisons to cure, toxins to detoxify and dilutes drugs so much that the original substance is untraceable in any scientific analysis.

The origins of homoeopathy go back to 1810 when a German physician called Samuel Hahnemann first proposed a new system of medicine as an alternative to the orthodox practices of the day. These included bloodletting and purging, which Dr Hahnemann considered too harsh, and which often weakened the patients more than their illnesses. By contrast the new system was to be based on gentler ways of helping the body to heal itself.

Dr. Hahnemann's ideas were inspired by the discovery that a herbal remedy against malaria, made from cinhona tree bark, produced symptoms of malaria such as headache and fever, when taken by a healthy person. He concluded that symptoms were the body's way of fighting illness and that medicines which produced the same symptoms as the illness could aid recovery (it was later discovered that cinhona bark contains quinine, the first drug used against malaria).

Samuel Hahnemann's ideas were, in effect, a re-discovery of an ancient principle first expressed by the Greek physician Hippocrates in the fifth century BC. It can be summed up by the Latin words *similia similibus* curentur which translate as *likes cure like*. Dr. Hahnemann called the new system *homoeopathy* meaning *like disease* in contrast to conventional medicine which he termed *allopathy* meaning *against disease* since the latter uses medicines to suppress or prevent symptoms.

The law of dual effect - that of action and reaction - applies throughout nature and is the very foundation of healing science. It relates to and governs every phenomenon of health, disease and cure. What is commonly called a crisis, acute reaction or acute disease is, in reality, nature's attempt to establish health. Every agent affecting the human organism produces two effects - a first, but temporary, effect followed by a second lasting effect.

An example of this is the first, but temporary, effect of cold water applied to the skin which results in blood going to the interior of the body. The second effect is for the body to compensate for the local depletion by sending greater quantities of blood back to the surface resulting in increased warmth and better surface circulation. Conversely, the first effect of a hot bath is to draw blood to the surface (reddening it) but the secondary effect sends the blood back to the interior, leaving the surface bloodless and chilled.

Stimulants produce their deceptive effects by consuming the reserve stores of vital energy in the organism. This is inevitably followed by weakness and exhaustion in exact proportion to the previous excitation. The first effect of relaxation and sleep is weakness and half consciousness (the feeling when we first wake up) but this is followed by the secondary effect (when we are fully awake) which is an increase in vitality.

This dual effect applies to all drug action. The first temporary, violent effect of poisonous drugs is usually due to nature's efforts to overcome and eliminate these substances. For instance, if one takes a purgative the body will respond by trying to throw it out of the system and thus the first effect is to cause a bowel movement. The secondary, but lasting, effect is less welcome as continued use of purgatives is likely to cause constipation. This secondary effect is due to the retention of drug poisons in the system and their destructive action on the organism.

In theory and in practice allopathy considers the first effect only and ignores the lasting after-effects of drugs and surgical operations. It administers remedies whose first effect is contrary to the symptoms of the disease condition. Therefore, in accordance with the law of action and reaction, which are equal (well nearly equal according to the latest findings in quantum physics) but opposite, the second and lasting effect of such remedies must be similar to the disease condition.

Laxatives have already been mentioned - where the temporary irritation and overstimulation of the sensitive membranes of the digestive organs are followed by corresponding weakness and exhaustion. If this procedure is repeated often enough it becomes habitual. As discussed earlier the continued use of stimulants or tonics will eventually cause complete exhaustion and a reduction of physical and mental ability. Opiates, sedatives and hypnotics may give temporary relief but, if the original condition is due to constitutional causes, the result will be a worsening of the condition and possible addiction to the drug. Each drug breeds new disease symptoms which, in turn, are treated by other poisons and the vicious cycle continues.

On the other hand, the teaching and practice of homoeopathy is fully in harmony with the law of dual effect (action and reaction). Letting *likes cure like* it administers remedies in minute doses whose first, but temporary, effect, is similar to the disease condition but whose second, and lasting, effect must be contrary to it - and thus curative.

Dr. Hahnemann considered that small doses of homoeopathic remedies would be safer than large ones - whilst still being effective. He spent many years experimenting on himself, his family and his friends with a wide range of natural substances in dilute form. His approach was *holistic* because it took into consideration the *whole person - that is to say their physical, mental and emotional states.* Homoeopathic remedies are aimed at restoring natural balance to the body thus boosting its vital force and facilitating the fight against *dis*-ease.

Over the years Dr Hahnemann, by close observation and experiment, established three significant principles of homoeopathy. These are:
1)   that a medicine, which in large doses produces symptoms of a disease, will in small doses cure that disease.
2)   that by extreme dilution the medicine's curative properties are improved and all the poisonous or undesirable side effects are lost.

3)   that the medicines need to be prescribed individually by the study of the whole person which includes temperament, emotions and general constitution,

To give the reader an idea of how this works let me give a brief summary of the provings for the following three well-known homoeopathic remedies.

COFFEE in excess will produce excitability, sleeplessness, headaches, restlessness, palpitations and a variety of other symptoms. In homeopathic form, for certain individuals, it can be used to calm and aid sleep.

ARSENIC in significant doses would cause restlessness, burning pains, fear, cold sweat, thirst, diarrhoea, etc. A person demonstrating some of these symptoms, who fits this homoepathic picture, could be cured by arsenic in homoeopathic potency.

DEADLY NIGHTSHADE otherwise known as BELLA-DONNA in significant doses will cause heat, redness, throbbing or burning pains and dilated pupils amongst other symptoms but, unlike arsenic, no anxiety or fear. In homoeopathic strength it can be used to restore somebody demonstrating these symptoms.

HOMOEOPATHY treats the whole person, acknowledges the presence of microbes, does not name diseases, gives minute doses, stimulates self healing and tests its remedies on humans (provings). On the other hand ALLOPATHY treats symptoms only, looks on microbes as a cause, names diseases, gives large doses, is suppressive and tests on animals.

The average patient who visits a homoeopath for the first time is often somewhat mystified by the ensuing interview because most homoepaths take a rather different approach to the patient than does the average orthodox doctor. A good homoeopath will have a very personal approach to the patient because he is concerned with the whole person rather than with the clinical symptoms of a specific disease. He is *treating the patient rather than the disease.*

Homoeopathic philosophy accepts that there is a basic force within the patient often referred to as the life force. The absence of it would be seen as the difference between a living and a dead body. The life force is the very essence of the patient and it is this force that controls the health of the individual. Disease is *dis-ease;* a condition in which the body is out of harmony with itself and where this vital force is diminished.

The reason for this dis-harmony may be due simply to the strains and stresses of modern life taking their toll. It might be due to an accidental injury or progressive poisoning of the body with toxins of one sort or another. Perhaps it is the outcome of long term drug treatment or it might be due to an inherited weakness, or miasm, as it is called in homoeopathic terms? It might be a combination of many things.

The homoeopath acknowledges that the human body is basically a self-healing mechanism and the less interference this mechanism suffers the better it will function. The life force has enormous potential and the homoeopathic remedy needs to influence and resonate with it in order to stimulate and encourage the body to heal itself. As previously suggested the principle of dilution is essential to the administration of homoeopathic remedies or, to use the homoeopathic term, *potentisation.*

Minute doses of the original substance are used and, in some mysterious way, the more diluted or *potentised* the remedy, the more powerful it becomes.

What are the remedies? They can be animal, vegetable or mineral. Homoeopaths do use herbs and botanical medicines but usually only after potentisation. Apart from the drugs mentioned above, substances which in their natural state have little or no obvious effect on the human body such as sand, charcoal, common salt or pencil lead develop, in their potentised form, powerful healing properties in the right patient.

For the technically minded potencies of homeopathic medicines are prepared by mixing 1 part of the original substance, if in a liquid state, with 99 parts of rectified spirit. Insoluble substances are first ground up, or *triturated* and then mixed with sugar of milk in similar proportions. This first potentisation is known as a 1C potency (1 centesimal or 1 part in 100). During the process the mixture is thoroughly *succussed* by repeatedly banging it on a hard surface for a specific length of time. To make a 2C potency it is necessary to mix 1 part of the 1C dilution with a further 99 parts. A 3C potency is made with 1 part of this mixture with a further 99 parts and so on. The *succussion* process is continued whilst mixtures are being prepared. The centesimal scale was used by Hahnemann but a decimal scale (1 part in 10) was introduced at a later date and is indicated by the letter X after a potency e.g. 6X. Both scales are in use today.

The important point to remember about homoeopathic medicines is that they are incredibly minute. For example a 3C potency amounts to 1 part of the original substance *diluted* a *million* times. That is a *low* potency in homeopathic medicine and it is apparent, therefore, that whatever the effect of a homoeopathic remedy it is certainly not the physical content of it. Clearly such potentised remedies work at a very subtle level.

The patient has to realise that he cannot push all the responsibility for a cure on to the practitioner but must work with him to climb the slope to recovery. Homoeopathy is essentially natural healing with the remedy assisting the patient to regain health by stimulating nature's vital forces. Adequate rest and appropriate diet in a satisfactory environment will assist the process. It is, perhaps, very close to spiritual medicine and, indeed, some people call it a blend of science and magic! There is still a lot which is not fully understood about the workings of homoeopathy but most homoeopaths see enough evidence of remarkable changes in their patients to know they are using a system which, by and large, gives excellent results.

In some ways, homoeopathy is a bit like electricity in the sense that we know how to use the power quite successfully but nobody seems to know exactly what it is! Like many things the more one knows about homoeopathy the more one realises how much more there is to know.

6

HYPNOSIS

Imagination is more important than knowledge.
Einstein

When a person is in hypnosis the individual is physically relaxed and mentally alert. It is a very useful state. It allows for a particular form of communication between two people. Hypnosis is not something one person *does* to another but is based on an ability, which most people have, to *collaborate* in a particular way. Like all talents some people will have more ability than others to hypnotise and be hypnotised but everybody has the capacity to improve their innate capability by training and experience.

Hypnotising oneself is known as auto-hypnosis or self-hypnosis. This is simply a term of convenience because, in fact, all hypnosis is self-hypnosis. The ability of an individual to concentrate and use their imagination is crucial and this will produce what we call the *hypnotic effect*. It cannot be done without the co-operation of the person concerned. Thus to go into hypnosis requires a conscious decision. One can choose to go into it and, likewise, choose to come out of it *at any time.*

One is fully awake while hypnotised and aware of their surroundings. The more the individual allows relaxation to take place the more the surroundings fade into insignificance. A similar situation prevails when a person is absorbed in an engrossing film at the cinema where there is a lack of awareness of the theatre and of the other people in it. In the cinema there is no danger in allowing the imagination to run riot and in exactly the same way one is in no danger in becoming engrossed by the imagination while in hypnosis. If there was a fire alarm at the cinema, an unwelcome touch or some other disturbance one would immediately come out of that hypnotic state.

Familiar to most of us are the everyday trances we experience when listening to music, whilst ironing, watching television or, occasionally, even when driving a car. In each of these everyday situations we are pleasantly *in our imagination,* focused on thoughts and images created by ourselves or suggested by others.

Hypnosis is entirely safe but it can be misused through ignorance or malice. A person in hypnosis will only do what he or she believes to be right. However one must be aware that some people, whether in or out of hypnosis, can easily be persuaded to do things against their best interest. There are stories of people being fooled into self-harm whilst in hypnosis and the following one concerning a doctor who was reported to have *murdered* his wife is interesting:

Some years ago a physician/hypnotherapist, who was having an extramarital affair with a woman he wanted to marry, hypnotised his wife and suggested to her that she was developing a headache. He further suggested that the headache would become very severe and when it did so she would swallow all

the pills he had put into her lap. They would make her fall
asleep so that she would no longer be aware of the pain. After
a while she reached for the pills and took them all. It was a
lethal dose.

One wonders how this case ever came to light unless the perpetrator of the crime bragged about it. In any event if the story is true it was, of course, an immense breach of trust on the part of the doctor and reflects on his integrity rather than implicating the process of hypnotherapy.

On the other side of the coin hypnotherapists can be misguided by their patients. There is nothing to stop a person in hypnosis from lying about any experience they may have had and by so doing completely mislead the therapist.

People consciously experiencing hypnosis for the first time have varied impressions. Some will believe that they have not been in hypnosis at all whilst others will feel they have been deeply hypnotised and, for the remainder, the experience will be somewhere in between. Certain people have a tendency to go into *deep hypnosis* and may not remember what happened during the session. This is quite rare and estimated at only 3% of the population. However, studies show that even those people with such ability to be hypnotised, known as *somnambulates,* are protected by a *hidden observer* within themselves monitoring all that is happening. This keeps them safe and they will accept only those suggestions that they would find reasonable in their fully conscious state. Being in hypnosis is usually very pleasant and most people like to repeat the experience.

The most common view of hypnosis is that it is an altered state of consciousness in which the awareness differs, in some measure, to everyday reality. Another view is that it is a heightened state of suggestibility, but as already stated some people are very suggestible without being in hypnosis. The advertising industry is dependent on the fact!

Being in hypnosis is not some sort of stupor in which one is dependent on the hypnotherapist although, it is fair to say, there is a pleasing sense of relaxation. However, the suggestion that hypnosis is simply profound relaxation, and nothing more, has been refuted in laboratory studies which appear to prove otherwise. For example - after hypnosis the heart rate remains slowed down for longer than after relaxation alone.

It has also been suggested that whilst in hypnosis people act in a way which they think is expected of them, having been conditioned by what they have seen on television, at a stage show, or based on what they have read. This theory falls down when you consider the number of people who have experienced surgical operations in a hypnotic state and experienced no pain at all.

Our autonomic nervous system is intimately linked with the subconscious. Think of all the bodily functions such as breathing, blood circulation, digestion and so on. These functions can be deliberately controlled once hypnosis gives us access. Thus hypnosis can be used to lower blood pressure, reduce pulse rate, improve digestion, speed up healing or send blood to a particular area that needs warming and so on.

Because hypnosis requires the by-passing of the critical mind and the acceptance of selective thinking fear and doubt, which requires conscious negative thoughts, can prevent a person from entering hypnosis. There is more than a simple biological effect involved in hypnosis. It is the powerful effect of the link between the patient and the practitioner. As in most alternative therapies, there is a *special relationship between therapist and client which is most important.* This relationship may take time to develop.

I have already touched on some misconceptions about hypnosis. The comment *I don't think I was hypnotised because I heard every word you said* is typical and reflects that a person is awake and alert in hypnosis. Apart from the myth that hypnosis *is the same as sleep* there are several other common misconceptions about it. Examples are that *the client's mind is taken over by the hypnotist, that nothing will be remembered and that one is in some kind of oblivion.*

It is probably worth mentioning stage shows because they foster a lot of the misunderstandings about hypnosis. The participants are hypnotised but they are only doing what they want to do. For some participants it is a chance to demonstrate their exhibitionist tendencies, or to grab the opportunity to shed their inhibitions. The hypnotist can then be blamed for their temporary lapse in normal behaviour!

How does one know if one has been in hypnosis in a therapy session? Two or more of the following indications would suggest a person has experienced hypnosis:

deep physical relaxation
a feeling of non concern about time passing
fluttering eyelids
loss of sense of time
limbs feeling unusually heavy
everyday concerns fading
limbs feeling unusually light

alleviation of pain
imagined scenes seem real
feeling a tingling sensation
eyes watering
face appears smoothed
enjoying a deep sigh
nearby sounds seem distant
it feels OK to allow a surge of emotion
a pleasant sense of unreality
strong conviction that a goal can be achieved

Everyone can be hypnotised if they so choose. Indeed everyone goes into a light form of hypnosis every day of their lives. Day-dreaming is a form of hypnosis. Try closing your eyes now and then imagine the last person with whom you had a conversation and the circumstances in which you found yourself. Just see what details you can recall. Now open your eyes. Probably you were able to recall quite a lot. You have just experienced a light form of hypnosis and if you were helped into a deeper state your vision would be more focused and accurate.

Hypnosis is an uncomplicated, simple and extremely useful natural self-healing process.

7

HEALING

Every physical disability arises from some disharmony in the
soul, some lack of balance or emotional conflict.
White Eagle

We are all healers. Some people seem unaware of this whereas
others make an effort to develop their healing ability. When a
child falls down and hurts some part of its anatomy the first thing
the mother does is to pick up the child and probably run a
soothing hand over the injured part. This is healing. She does
it automatically. How often have you put a hand out to touch
a friend in need of comfort? This, too, is healing.

It is important to keep our physical bodies healthy by living in
harmony with natural and divine law. When these laws are
broken through some lapse on our part, we suffer. The body
needs to be treated with respect and consideration and, indeed
to be loved. If we are to do this we had best not overwork,
overstrain, overfeed or over-indulge ourselves in any way. It is
our responsibility to care for our physical vehicle by treating it
kindly.

Every physical disability arises from some disharmony in the soul, some lack of balance or emotional conflict. The idea is, perhaps, unpalatable to many of us. We do not like to admit that our sickness is due to some imbalance or fault within ourselves. Lack of harmony in our thoughts and in our lives brings *dis-ease* whereas harmony brings health so it is important to let go of all resentment, fear or criticism.

Basically all healing is the intake into the body of the eternal sun, the light. We need to call upon this light, breathe it in, see it and live consciously in it. We are so encumbered with our heavy physical bodies and so attached to material life that we can be forgiven for overlooking the fact that we can recreate the very cells and tissues of our bodies by harnessing our thoughts in an imaginative and positive way.

Trained healers work in a variety of ways. There are many techniques but the important ingredient is unconditional love. It is helpful to visualise the healing energy coming through from a higher source. Simply using one's own energy can be depleting - which is both undesirable and unnecessary. Assuming that the healer, at the time of offering the healing, is stronger than the recipient then he is able to receive more fully that divine light, that spiritual force. The healer, via one or more of the chakras (more on this later) causes the light to be stimulated in the recipient.

In contact healing, which is to say when the person requiring help is with you, one simple technique is to imagine or visualise in your mind divine light, which is energy, coming into you from the sun. See this force pouring into your body and then think of yourself as a transformer converting it into a form which is acceptable to the person who has asked for help. Visualise the divine light permeating your whole being and then going out from your heart centre and then through your hands so that the flow can be directed to the required area.

This same healing thought (thought is energy) can be used at a distance. You do not have to have a person next to you in order to give them healing. Simply visualise the person to whom you wish to send a healing thought and that healing energy will be with the person immediately. Distance is of no importance. It is like saying a prayer for somebody you love and it is instantaneous.

As indicated above, the technique is not so vital as the unconditional love and the simple but clear thought which goes into it. It is worth having in mind a picture, or visualisation, for instant use at any convenient moment when the need is there. By this I mean the sort of visualisation previously suggested. See your body acting as a transformer of light from the sun and let your heart centre act as a lighthouse sending out a beam of light to the individual in need.

To be healed spiritually means that the spirit is able to fill the physical body and the soul body with light. If you could see with your inner vision when a healer is at work you would see a light emanating from their finger tips and radiating from the whole body. This spiritual light is the instrument of the healing power and it is generated by love. The disharmony behind a particular illness might be so subtle that it is difficult to recognise the cause. Most of us are guilty of breaking spiritual laws, on a regular basis, so it is not surprising that our bodies show the strain from time to time because overstraining our physical, emotional or mental bodies is a common cause of illness.

What about the saints in the world who, apparently, undergo dreadful suffering? One might wonder where the disharmony or conflict is in these souls? To find the cause of the suffering of today we would probably need to go back further than one life to find the answer. It might be the final outworking and *balancing of the books f*or some error long in the past. Or it might be that they have chosen to work through a crippled body as their gift to the world? So far as healing is concerned we ought not to separate one life from another. It is helpful to look upon the chain of lives as one continuous story or think of the various lives as chapters in a long book.

The concept of *karma* and *reincarnation* (more on this in later chapters) is relevant. Where does one stand with healing if bodily suffering and sickness are due to the outworking of *karma?* Very briefly, *karma* is an eastern word used to describe the inexorable law of cause and effect. In biblical terms it is covered by the phrase - *as one sows so one reaps.* Is it right to help sufferers to overcome such *karma* by giving spiritual healing? I think it is. We have to do our best to help and heal those who ask for or need assistance.

The parable of the good Samaritan illustrates this point. In that parable, Jesus advises us to love our neighbours as ourselves. When asked by a lawyer - *who is my neighbour?* - Jesus talked about a man who had been stripped, beaten and left half dead by robbers on the road from Jerusalem to Jericho. This unfortunate was ignored by a priest and a Levite but greatly helped by the Samaritan who rendered every assistance.

What part does the patient have to play in such healing? The individual is being offered a magnificent opportunity, originating from his *good karma* to rise above the affliction of body and soul. If the man is wise he will respond to the opportunity and endeavour to learn the lesson which is proffered. In this way, by aspiring to the highest instinct, the *karma* is worked out or *transmuted.*

The natural physical instinct is to fear but we need to learn that no harm can touch the real person within. There is nothing to fear except fear itself. If we have complete confidence in our Maker then light will flow through our being and all darkness will be eliminated. Just remember that where there is light there can be no darkness!

All human life is governed by divine law and, necessary though it may be to endure pain whilst in a physical body, it is to be hoped that we will do so with courage. The problems with which we are faced, if looked upon as an opportunity from which to learn wisdom, will be more easily borne. We have to remember that, in accordance with the law of cause and effect or *karma,* the sufferer has at some time sown the seed for the current experiences. Thus there is little point in blaming God or, for that matter, anybody else!

8

WHENCE WHITHER AND WHY?

All the world's a stage
And all the men and women merely players.
William Shakespeare

Why are we here? Why indeed? What is the purpose of life?
Who started it all and why? There is no easy answer. Since life
is an eternal business there is no starting point and no end. We
are on a seemingly unending journey. Already it has been a long
voyage.

But why this journey? Why leave heavenly bliss to journey
downwards into matter and then have to struggle back to the
world of light? I suggest the spirit of man, that divine energising
spark of life, descends into action through various planes of
consciousness. Finally it reaches the physical and creates about
itself the body, or that aspect of us, we call the soul. This is the
familiar ourself of feelings, likes, dislikes, interests, affections,
memories and sentiments. Soul is a word for we ourselves living
inside the outer man looking out through our eyes, speaking
with our tongue and lips and thinking with our brain. It is this
ourself which survives death and then migrates to a higher realm
(see chapter 13).

Man started, pure and innocent, originally breathed forth from the womb of love, wisdom and power. It may help to think of creation as a *breathing-out* of the breath of God and think of the rhythm of life as a mighty *out-breathing and in-breathing* of the Creator. The whole of creation - including the mineral, vegetable, animal, human and angelic kingdoms result from this *out-breathing and in-breathing* of the divine intelligence.

So far as man is concerned the journey is to learn about conquering weakness, controlling matter and overcoming temptation. This can only be learned in the dense surroundings of planet earth and is the reason why we are here We have come thus far as unconscious, but potentially divine, sparks from the Godhead. The route, or descent, might be a better word, has been through levels of life invisible to present day man. A vast descent through many layers taking on ever heavier clothing until such time that we are in a body of dense flesh and in a material environment and existence.

As the spirit descends it becomes individualised and in the process gains experience. When it is in its densest form, it seems entirely preoccupied in its own self or personality and concerned only for its own pleasure or power. Gradually, but inexorably, the burden increases until the soul reaches the lowest arc of its evolution and is completely immersed in dense material life, This is the most dense and heavy form man will ever know. We are here on earth and encased in matter. Our physical body is the crudest form in which our life can be expressed.

If the soul did not descend into the darkness of matter its latent powers and consciousness of God would not be realised. It is only under the pressure of the stresses and strains of life on earth that the soul gradually evolves. Think of a seed in the darkness of the earth which bursts forth under the influence of rain, warmth and sunlight. In the long descent into dense material life beauty and truth, to which the soul will eventually return, is not part of its awareness. The innate goodness now dormant in every human soul has to be stimulated. Man needs to become aware that all the secrets of the universe are hidden within his own being.

The great journey back home starts when man turns his face towards the heavenly light. In our physical bodies we have to work really hard to unfold spiritually and make the road back into the heavenly state. Whatever we sow we reap. Our thoughts, words and actions are having their effects on a daily basis. On the earth plane the soul must overcome the weakness of the flesh to master its emotions. This is essential to its purpose. Having achieved self-mastery then it is free. Free because it has become fully God-conscious. In these circumstances man is at one with the divine whilst still on earth.

Most people imagine that the personality they know on the physical plane is all of them. Not so. It is only a very small part of the whole that is imprisoned in physical life. If we visualise a triangle with the base in the heavens and the point downwards to the earth then what manifests through the body is the point of the triangle. That small earthly part is here as a messenger, a seeker, to gather experience in the flesh. God-consciousness is able to manifest through the very narrow channel which we know as our personality.

In esoteric literature we often read that man was once a far more spiritual being than he is today and also that there were God-men on the earth in a long forgotten age. Some will have read of the legends of Atlantis and perhaps even of existences before that era. If God-men dwelt on earth long ago why is man, apparently, still at so low a state of spiritual consciousness? Man descended from his high estate in accordance with the divine plan. He had to undergo a process of gradual descent to inhabit a physical vehicle. That vehicle had evolved from a lower state of life, stage by stage, until the brain had developed to such a degree that it could begin to comprehend the God within. Man contains God, the divine essence, within his own soul. However, it takes a long time for that seed of God, that divine essence or part of God, to manifest through to our physical consciousness and general awareness.

The planets of the solar system were born from the sun and the birth of man is related to the birth of the solar system. The condition of the earth's surface in those days was very different - in the beginning the earth was in a gaseous condition. Early man possessed a body, a vehicle, adapted to the conditions of the earth planet at that time. Try to think of man in a state of life before he developed his higher powers of action and thought. At that time the physical body would not be like the one to which we are accustomed now. The spirit, or consciousness, was more outside than within the body. The spirit was still existing in a higher state of life.

There had to be a process of creating a physical vehicle and also a way of developing all the subtler bodies which clothe the spirit of man. Gradually the mind, brain and body of man evolved until such time there was a vehicle through which the divine light might descend. In perfect man full consciousness of the divine life is able to manifest. Man has spent many ages developing his physical body and that body is still evolving. When such bodies reach a point at which the spirit of man can no longer gain in spiritual consciousness the vehicle commences to degenerate and fall away. This is illustrated in the dying-out of various races to make way for beings with ever finer bodies. Bodies more sensitive, more attuned and more able to develop spiritual attributes - thanks to the consciousness of other planes of being.

In this process of evolution, as the soul begins to absorb the light pouring on it from the divine, it turns to climb upward again. From the depths of materialism the soul turns once again to the light. The layers of earthiness and selfishness are cast aside as the real nature starts to assert itself - urging the soul and spirit on to become the radiant being that God intended. The soul develops from unconsciousness to consciousness and through the ages it grows - ultimately to become master of matter, of itself and conscious of the light and love of God.

The earth substance, in its own descent, has long been crystal-lising and solidifying. It, too, is on a long journey. At this time the earth together with the human soul and spirit have touched the bottom of the descending arc. We are more than a physical body and we will not, or rather cannot, die. The whole purpose of life and evolution can be summed up as growth *from unconsciousness through self-consciousness to God-consciousness.* This is the grand plan but whilst it is being fulfilled we need to be patient and keep the faith.

9

SPIRITUALITY VERSUS RELIGION

*He who wears his morality but as his best garment were better
naked.*
Kahlil Gibran

There seems to be some confusion between religion and spirituality. According to my Oxford dictionary *RELIGION* is defined
as: *recognition of superhuman controlling power and especially of a personal God or Gods entitled to obedience and
worship, effect of such recognition on conduct or mental
attitude; particular system of faith and worship. SPIRITUAL-
ITY* is defined as: *spiritual quality. SPIRIT* is defined as: *the
animating or vital principle, intelligent or immaterial part of
man, soul; person viewed as possessing this, especially with
reference to particular mental or moral qualities.*

In my experience religion has caused more than a few difficulties
and it tends to tie us to *DOGMA* which is defined as: *an arrogant
declaration of opinion.* On that basis religion seems to be the
way we go about practising dogma, whereas spirituality is
something more ethereal and refers to a higher, if less tangible,
part of our being. Sometimes I feel that we lose sight of our

spirituality when we get bogged down into a particular religion or dogma.

As mentioned previously the religious faiths that comforted our fathers will not necessarily suffice for the modern generation. It was thought unseemly to ask too many awkward questions in the past but, in this day and age, no such constraints apply. For all that some of the standard answers to *awkward* questions on religious matters are less than satisfactory. If one asks the average priest what happens when we die one may find the answer a little vague and, in my opinion, not especially comforting. Do we really sit at God's right hand where *there are pleasures for evermore. (Psalms 17:11)?* Or do we simply sit on a cloud strumming a harp? Or, perhaps, spend eternity shovelling coal into some diabolical furnace?

For an individual brought up in a particular faith or religion it is difficult to opt out of that belief. After all, as children, we believe what we are told by our parents and teachers. We listen to what they say and read the books that are presented to us thus perpetuating those beliefs. As we get older we may wonder about the validity of some of these things. It depends, to some extent, on how seriously religion is taken in our particular household. There is a tendency for people of like mind to mix together and thus those of a given persuasion are likely to have that view reinforced rather than questioned.

In the West the predominant religion is Christianity. This is echoed by the church and, in some cases, by the state. Other religions are tolerated but, I suspect, they are looked upon as inferior. However, for an individual brought up as a Buddhist or Muslim or Hindu or whatever, the situation would be different. They would, presumably, consider their belief to be correct and those of the Christian, or other religion, to be false in some way. Clearly, our beliefs depend upon our upbringing, geographical location and environment.

I am not trying to belittle the belief of any individual. In my view any religion that gives comfort or helps a person to lead a happy and constructive life is good. However, I am trying to make the point that it is not a bad idea to stand back and look at one's inherited beliefs with detachment and to consider the possibility that the *inherited view* may not be as well founded as one might like to think.

In this connection I must make the point that the leaders of the Christian church changed the rules in AD553 when, at the Council of Constantinople, it was agreed by a majority that anybody who supported *the mythical doctrine of pre-existence of the soul and who believed in the soul's return to earth after death should henceforth be anathema.* Anathema is defined as: *an accursed thing, curse of God, curse of the Church, excommunication; imprecation.* Take your pick but, put in simple terms, it meant that anybody who believed in reincarnation after that date was in for a hard time! In this way the church leaders suppressed a truth that had been taught in the mystery schools throughout the ancient world. It is one of the fundamental confusions about Christianity.

Surely there has to be more to life than birth, seventy years or so of trials and tribulations, death and departure? Anyway, where do people go when they die? Does it depend on religious belief? Since there are countless religions there must be countless places to go? Perhaps? What happens if we are not religious? Is there nowhere to go? Is there life after death? I have already touched on reincarnation. Is there any proof that we have been here before? Has our health and well-being anything to do with spirituality and the kind of life we lead? The answers to these questions are available to us all if we care to do a little research. Hopefully, this book will suggest some answers and provide some food for thought about such issues.

I like to think that I am a *Christian* but I have already nailed my colours to the mast in acknowledging all the evidence in favour of the concept of reincarnation. Following the decision at the Council of Constantinople AD553 that makes me an *accursed thing*. This is a pity but I can live with it because I think the decision was a nonsense designed, at the time, to perpetuate the power of the priests and keep the masses in their place. The fact of the matter is that we are really *spirit people doing a stint on earth* rather than the other way round. The greatest mistake we make is to think of ourselves as separate from God or from the universe into which we have been born. We are all part of the one whole.

In my understanding God, the eternal spirit is both Father and Mother and the Son is the Christ Light which shines in the hearts of all people. The significance of the Light and its connection with the First Born or Son of God is very important and this is discussed in a later chapter.

10

GREAT TEACHERS

*To arrive at truth you must become very humble, very simple in
yourself. The great people are those who are simple in heart.*
White Eagle

Throughout the history of life on earth, in all races, in all parts
of the world, spiritual teachers have come to help people in the
way most needed at the time. Many of those teachers are known
by the great religions which have grown out of their teachings.

The *Ancient Wisdom* teachings, contained in collections of
books and documents as well as being in the collective unconscious of the human race, have come from the scriptures of all
religions. It is the name given to the truths about God and
creation which were brought to earth many thousands of years
ago by wise spiritual teachers. Let us look at some of these
teachers and consider what they had to tell us.

KRISHNA

Some of the oldest teachings come from Krishna who was born
in India about 3,000 years before Jesus of Nazareth. Reportedly
a very happy child who spent a lot of time singing and dancing

with the cowherds. Krishna was always smiling, full of joy and laughter.

As he grew up he realised that not everybody was so happy and he spent many years experiencing the pain and suffering of others to find out why this should be the case. Finally, in a forest hermitage, so the legend goes, he met a great Rishi (spiritual teacher) who explained to him that all life is one. Everything from the lowest insect to the greatest king is part of the same life, part of God. The teacher explained that the unhappiness of the people was because, in their hearts, they were unaware of this great truth.

The Rishi told Krishna that he had a very special mission in the world which was to bring this knowledge to other people by the example of his own life. Krishna did this very thing and many people in India followed him on this joyful path. He is still much revered there and elsewhere in the world. The teachings of Krishna that were given to his beloved disciple Arjuna are contained in a book called the *Bhagavad Gita* meaning *The Lord's Song*. Krishna is frequently depicted dancing and playing the flute and bringing joy and happiness into the world.

MOSES

The story of Moses is told in the Old Testament of the Bible. At one time all Hebrew babies were ordered to be killed by a ruthless Pharaoh (Egyptian king), thought to be Rameses II, who is believed to have lived from about 1292 BC to 1225 BC. Moses was hidden in the rushes on the banks of the river Nile and it is here that he was found by that same Pharaoh's daughter. When he grew up, to be a leader of his people, he became aware of God talking to him. The story goes that this first happened when he saw *a great fire in the bushes* although the flames did not burn anything. He knew he had to lead his people, known as the children of Israel, out of Egypt, where they were being cruelly treated as slaves, to safety in the promised land.

Before they could leave Egypt the country was swept with plagues and other disastrous events, supposedly brought about by God to encourage the Pharaoh to allow them to leave. When they finally escaped from Egypt they wandered for a long time in the wilderness. However, when they were hungry God sent *manna* for them to eat. During this time Moses was summoned to the top of Mount Sinai to receive the ten commandments in the form of tablets of stone. On descending from the mountain top he found his people worshipping a golden calf. He thought they had forgotten about God, or Jehovah, as they called Him. Moses was so angry that he broke the stone tablets listing the commandments. Later, however, he went up the mountain again and, after 40 days and 40 nights, returned with new tablets. In due course his people did behave as they had been instructed and just before Moses died, at the ripe old age of 120, he was shown *the promised land* to which he had so faithfully led his people.

There is a symbolic interpretation of the story of Moses. *The promised land* - the heavenly world; *plagues, etc.* - the tests earth life brings; *the wilderness* - lost in the sense of the desire for material things; *manna* - spiritual food; *top of the mountain* - aspiration to God; *ten commandments* - spiritual law for life on earth and in heaven; *golden calf* - material things.

The commandments, of course, give instructions to help people behave in a kind and brotherly way to one another and to love God (or good) more than earthly things (Mammon). The Jews, who are the descendants of the children of Israel, try to put what they see as God's law (the Torah) into practice in their lives. They believe that by following the law with a pure heart and giving devotion to God in prayer, one can be directly in touch with the Creator.

BUDDHA

Siddharta Gautama Buddha was born a prince (son of a raja) in India 563 years before Christ. He was brought up in a palace surrounded by great luxury but there was a cloud hanging over the household. This was a prophecy about what would happen if the prince saw anybody sick, old or dead, or if he saw a holy man. For this reason his father, the king, tried to keep him from seeing what life was really like. He allowed the prince to see only beauty and happiness.

One day, having left the protected environment of the palace, the prince was helping the workers in the fields. Seeing the tender grass torn up covered with the eggs and little ones of insects which had been killed and scattered by the plough he was seized by a deep grief, as if he had helped to bring about the massacre of his own relations. And seeing the labourers with their complexions withered by the dust, by the intense heat of the sun and by the wind, the most noble of men was roused by a great compassion. He seated himself in the shade of a tree and meditated for the first time upon the grief of the world.

Thus the prophecy his father had feared was fulfilled. The prince saw people suffering and, later, met a holy man. He observed that the holy man was very calm and serene in spite of all the suffering around him. The prince was no longer content. At the age of 27 he left the palace and his family. He gave up his wealth to search out the meaning of life, death and suffering.

At first he followed a very strict and severe regime, nearly starving himself to death in the process. Later he realised that a moderate approach or *middle path* was better. Eventually, during a seven day meditation, he recalled many of his past lives and received his great awakening. He became Buddha, the enlightened one and spent the rest of his life helping people to understand *The Noble Eightfold Path* - right views, right motive, right speech, right action, right livelihood, right effort, right concentration and right contemplation. Thus the Buddhist faith preaches harmlessness. It also teaches that suffering is inseparable from existence and that the principle cause of suffering is desire. By the suppression of desire, via discipline, suffering can be avoided and ultimately Nirvana (extinction of individual existence and absorption into supreme spirit) achieved. Today hundreds of millions of people practise Buddhism in Asia and elsewhere.

CHINESE PHILOSOPHERS

Lao-Tzu, circa 604 BC to 524 BC, known as *the old philosopher* lived in China. As a child he learned about the Tao (universal harmony) or the way of the universe. He was told by his teacher that when everyone goes along with the Tao the world is at peace and everyone is happy. Lao-Tzu observed that many people did not understand or do this and he wrote an epic called *Tao Te Ching - The Book of the Right Way* to help them. This great work was read by a scholar called Chuang Tzu in 4BC who later wrote a more easily understood work about the Tao. This now famous book is called *Chuang Tzu* after his name.

Confucius, 550BC to 478BC, a contemporary of Buddha, who lived in China also tried to teach people how to behave so that everybody could live happily together. Confucius taught, with good sense and humour, the practice of the four virtues: equity, generosity, the observance of rites, and the discrimination between Good and Evil.

He advised the governors of the Chinese states and even the emperor, how they should rule the people. Confucius remarked that *everybody lives without paying attention to anyone else* and he suggested simple rules of love and loyalty. He and others collected the stories and wise sayings of old China and put them into books called the Chinese Classics. The *I Ching or Book of Changes* is the first of these and is one of the most important books in world's literature along with the *Bible, Bhagavad Gita and the Koran.*

ZEN

Zen has grown from Chinese philosophy merging with the teachings of Buddha. Zen has been practised in Japan since about AD1200 and students seek complete understanding of all creation, like Buddha's sudden awakening to truth, through discipline of mind and body. Enlightenment can come when doing ordinary everyday tasks. Zen masters teach their pupils by using curious riddles called Koans. These are designed to stop ordinary thoughts of the physical brain so that the higher mind and intuition can reveal a truth. This often happens suddenly in a flash of inner understanding. The following is an example of a famous Koan - a monk asked the Zen master, Joshu: *what is the principle of Buddha's teaching?* He received the reply *the cypress tree in the courtyard.* Make of that what you will!

JESUS OF NAZERETH

Jesus was prepared in many previous lives for his incarnation as a world teacher. He brought a very special blessing to the world. The Light, or Christ Spirit, shone through him in an extraordinary way. His teaching was that of love. Jesus did not want people to worship him but to worship God. His teaching abounds with expressions of unconditional love - *love God, love your neighbour as yourself, love your enemies, love one another.*

After Jesus' death his followers started to insist that only He was the Son of God and that people could only be saved by believing in Him. There is another point of view however, as discussed in a later chapter, and it is that people are saved, if that is the correct term, by their conduct in this life and acceptance of the Christ Light which shines in their own hearts. The ultimate goal of mankind is that this inner light should become so strong and radiant that even the cells of the physical body are transmuted into finer substances which can overcome mortality. This is known as the *Christing of Man,* or in the words of the *Ancient Brotherhood,* the *Blooming of the Rose upon the Cross of matter.*

Mohammed

Mohammed, born AD570, came after Jesus and founded the great world religion called Islam. He was born in Mecca, now in Saudi Arabia. Both his parents died when he was young and he was brought up by his uncle, a merchant in Mecca. At that time the people there believed in many gods and that the way to please them was to kill animals in holy places! However, as Mohammed grew up, he met people who were Christians and Jews and he became convinced that there was only one God. He started to meditate on his own in a quiet cave away from the hubbub of Mecca and, one day, he heard a voice saying *you are the messenger of Allah (God).*

During further meditations he saw the Angel Gabriel and was given many messages from God. Mohammed told people that they must submit to the will of Allah and by so doing they would arrive at an inner peace. This new religion was called Islam and many people began practising its teachings. Mohammed ran into trouble with the pagans in Mecca and in AD622 he fled to Medina, known as the city of the Prophet. This was the Hegira, the *year one* on the Mohammedan calendar. On the death of Mohammed in AD632, his successors, the Caliphs: Bakr, Omar, Othmann and Ali declared the *Holy Wars* to spread the teaching of the Prophet.

The great principles of the new religion of Islam were recorded by his disciples in the Koran (bible of Islam). Sufi teachers, incidentally, interpret the Koran from an inner spiritual point of view showing how to find God within the heart and revealing the oneness of all life.

SRI SATHYA SAI BABA

Sai Baba was born on November 23, 1926, in Puttapparthi, a remote village in central southern India. He is the fourth child of a humble and pious couple and has demonstrated evidence of his supernatural origins since the day of his birth. At age 14 he disclosed that he is the reincarnation of Shirdi Sai Baba. Sai Baba of Shirdi had lived the life of a Muslim fakir in the village of Shirdi in western India and laid the foundation for Hindu-Muslim unity in northern India by the example of his life and activities. Before his death in 1918 he prophesied his reincarnation in 8 years time.

Thousands of people have been and continue to be testimony to the supernatural powers of Sai Baba. He knows all of the Sacred Scriptures of every religion and converses with philosophers, doctors and scientists from all over the world, showing the depth of his knowledge in all the sciences: physical, metaphysical, and spiritual. He answers questions from his devotees before they have time to verbalise them. He knows the past, present and future of each person and often proves it. Sai Baba frequently appears at the same time in different places and hears the calls for help from his devotees all over the world thus saving them from danger or difficulty. He has the power to manipulate energy and can materialise objects out of nothing, change them or make them disappear. He can cure *incurable* illness and has power over the forces of nature.

Sri Sathya Sai Baba has descended as an Avatar (incarnation of God in human form) for all mankind and not for any particular community, religion or interest. His teachings are universal and not sectarian. Devotees, seekers and adherents of all faiths from all nationalities and countries find their way to him driven by the quiet conviction that they must encounter the Avatar and receive his blessing. He does not ask for veneration and is known to millions in the world simply as Baba. He instructs everyone to honour God in the way they feel best and in the manner they have been raised and taught, using the cult and the prayer of their own religion, *at least until the person transcends from the religious to the spiritual, passing from the outer search to an inner one.*

Thus the great teachers spread their messages to the world. How much distortion and complication has happened since then? How many wars have started over who has the *true* religion? How many *holy* wars have been fought? History shows us how man has used religion to further his own ends and yet the original messages were all about how to live happily and be kind to one another.

According to my understanding a very abbreviated summary of the messages of those great teachers might be as follows:

Krishna - be happy. Moses - worship God, not Mammon. Lao-Tzu - go with the flow. Confucius - love and loyalty. Zen - discipline brings enlightenment. Buddha - harmlessness. Jesus - love one another. Mohammed - oneness of all life. Sri Sathya Sai Baba - love all, serve all.

Where have we gone wrong?

11

GRACE COOKE AND WHITE EAGLE

Our whole aim is to help each one of you to unfold spiritual qualities, so that a sweet and serene communion between those in the spirit world and yourself becomes not only possible, but natural and right.
White Eagle

Since some of the content of this book has originated in the unseen or non-physical world I think it important that I explain a little more about the spiritual teacher known as White Eagle and something about clairvoyance.

White Eagle was the companion and spiritual teacher of Grace Cooke throughout her life and, indeed, through many incarnations. The teachings of White Eagle, one of the elder brethren, are reflected throughout the pages of this book and I quote his words directly on various pages. Elder brethren, by the way, are individuals who have experienced an elevation of consciousness. This has been brought about by attaining a level of spiritual consciousness which facilitates close communion with the Eternal Spirit. From such levels elder brethren work unceasingly for the spiritual illumination and unfoldment of humanity. Thanks to their close harmony with the Creator their own soul-

70

consciousness expands and they have the ability to become attuned to all human life. In this noble state they have the capacity to act as messengers between the Creator and his creatures.

Elder brethren have the ability to retain their physical form as men and women and are very close to humanity. They have a lot of experience of human life in all its states and grades and, in consequence, they have a great deal of understanding of the most elementary needs of any human being. They exude all pervading love and understanding. In their constant worship of God they radiate light and love to humanity. The ceaseless work and influence radiated by these great ones goes unrecognised by most of humanity. Elder brethren are never severe, hasty or judgmental. Instead they are endlessly patient and, knowing how slow the process of soul expansion is, they do not expect too much of anyone. How encouraging!

The name White Eagle, according to American Indian legend means a *spiritual teacher.* A white eagle is the symbol of the New Age of Aquarius and also of St. John. In the Ancient Mysteries the white eagle was a symbol for the higher psychic and spiritual powers of man indicating one who had clear sight, or clairvoyance, into the inner and secret worlds. According to one American Indian source the white eagle flies straight towards the sun which is an interesting remark to anybody who has studied the teachings of White Eagle.

Grace Cooke had received training in many lives and there is a deep attunement between her and White Eagle. As already stated the two were related in past incarnations and there is complete harmony and *at-one-ment* between them. This is detailed in a book called THE ILLUMINED ONES and in that story Grace Cooke tells about her life in South America as the daughter of *Hah-Wah-Tah,* an earlier incarnation of White Eagle, immortalised in the poem HIAWATHA by Longfellow.

White Eagle communicated regularly through Grace Cooke. At those times her own voice changed and the soothing tones of White Eagle were immediately recognisable. Recordings of White Eagle's teachings are stored at the White Eagle Lodge in Liss and the content of many of these messages is published regularly in books and journals.

It is believed that White Eagle once had an incarnation as an American Indian, who was a Maya chieftain, and it was in that guise that he usually presented himself to Grace Cooke. However, he has also appeared as a Tibetan, an Egyptian priest and a Pharaoh, as a humble brother of an obscure order and as an alchemist in the Middle Ages. He also had an important incarnation in France where the six-pointed star was used by the particular brotherhood he served. In Greece, as well as in Egypt, he lived as a teacher and philosopher. As a North American Indian he reached a great age and, according to his own story, was a chief among the Six Tribes. His mission then was to lead the Indians into brotherhood and peace amongst themselves.

Whatever bodies and personalities have been his in the past, followers today know him as *dear old White Eagle.* He has never been known to speak harshly or unkindly, judge nor condemn anyone. He always speaks with great optimism and with love and gentleness. The quality and depth of his knowledge, his understanding of human needs and the conviction with which he speaks, makes it clear that the information comes from a highly evolved being. White Eagle, of course, makes no such claim but reiterates that he is simply an instrument saying *only God is good, and He it is that doeth the work.*

The physical body of the average man is not very receptive to spiritual influences. In most people there is no consciousness of the etheric body. Certain people, however, have a loose etheric body which can slip out of the physical very easily. In such cases uncontrolled clairvoyance and obsession can result. There is a vast difference between this clairvoyance on the lower etheric plane and the correct use of psychic centres or chakras used by highly trained individuals.

Whilst incarnate and *imprisoned* here on earth there are subtle and refined states of life within the physical that may be penetrated. If true and clear messages are to come from spirit they can only be sent on a perfectly attuned line of communication and, in order to have some appreciation of how this might be accomplished, it is necessary to understand that we are not simply a physical body (see chapter 13).

The quality of clairvoyance or *clear vision* depends on many factors. There are many different forms of communication from the spirit world. In the past individuals who dealt with such matters were usually trained as priests or priestesses and were, in some degree, removed from the everyday world, living in seclusion, peace and meditation. It is an area fraught with difficulty and is not without danger. It is not something to be undertaken lightly. A lot of knowledge is required and anybody contemplating developing this ability should do so only under appropriate guidance.

If one imagines a still lake, with the reflection of trees and sky in the water, there is a beautiful calming effect. Conversely, if we imagine the lake in rough conditions, the reflection would be shattered. The reflection, or symbol, or play of light and colour was simply that - a reflection. If we then raise our eyes to the actual landscape we shall again see the trees and sky but this time something which is steady, clear and, to our senses, real. This is the difference between involuntary clairvoyance - which is often a reflection of an uncontrolled or undeveloped proceeding - and intelligent, trained clairvoyance receiving light or impetus from the plane of divine spirit.

I believe man is intended to soar from earthiness into these higher worlds of truth and light but the ability does not come easily. Such journeys, into the invisible realms, have been the inspiration for many philosophers, sages and saints through the ages. In a book called THE SHINING PRESENCE Grace Cooke describes such a journey of the soul. The following extract is taken from the chapter called *A Cave in the Mountains* and describes a significant meditation she experienced. It reads thus:

After a long period of training I was taken by the Shining Presence to his home in the invisible world. I seemed to rise like a bird and together we travelled, up and up, to what appeared to be a great height. The mists began to clear and I was able to see the surrounding country.

We had arrived at the edge of a great lake and the time was a little after sunrise. The air was as clear as crystal, the sun gently warmed the ground and ourselves. The silence and the harmony of the scene conveyed a deep and eternal peace which we also felt within our souls. The great mountain peaks rose, in some instances, sheer from the edge of the lake. The early morning shadows on the lake and mountains gave promise of unfolding beauty and radiance as the day advanced.

The canoe, which was waiting at the water's edge, was made of birch bark - it's curved ends gracefully shaped. We stepped into it and glided over the blue water which was so clear that the bottom of the lake was quite visible. Through this water another world danced before my eyes for at the bottom of the lake were beautiful plants with tiny but perfect flowers. In this water kingdom there were also many lovely coloured stones, glistening like jewels or precious gems.

Then I looked above the lake and saw the great pine trees towering on the shore towards which we were moving. They grew in dark green clumps on the mountain side where I could just see a little silver path winding up and up.

'Before we attempt the ascent' said White Eagle 'we will go to the shrine for rest and refreshment'. He took me by the hand and we went into a little cave. It was just a resting place; the ground was of silver sand strewn with moss, tiny plants and exquisite little shells. There were two places hollowed out in the ground to the shape of the human form and where the head could rest was a pillow of green moss. A little spring of water trickled through a naturally cut channel and drained itself into the lake. Cupping our hands we drank and refreshed ourselves at this crystal stream.

As we sat with legs crossed in the entrance to the cave, we gazed across the still deep blue lake, absorbing the cosmic light of the life-force which all nature was pouring out. I felt I wanted nothing more than to be allowed to sit in this beautiful spot. 'Is this heaven?' I asked.

'It is your heaven for the time being' said White Eagle. 'You must remember that heaven is a very vast place and even for you there may be many heavens; indeed any place which brings you complete harmony and a realisation of your union and at-onement with the cosmos is your heaven.'

'Then we do not necessarily have to journey far away from earth to find it?'

'No' said White Eagle 'Heaven is a state of conscious happiness which is realised by the soul in differing degrees. Heaven is anywhere where you are happy, according to your understanding of the moment. You may think heaven is a long way off but God intended that man should live in heaven on earth. In fact, when God created life, He put man into a state of heavenly bliss. The story of this, which has been handed down through long ages of earthly existence, can be read in symbolism in the Book of Genesis. It is sad that men have lost the secret of heaven and have now to spend countless ages in search of the key to the heavenly mysteries.'

'Will they ever find it now that they have descended so low into the earth?'

'Yes. They will find the lost key but only through the pain and the joy which human love brings. People often wonder how it is that God lets them suffer or why God permits so much tragedy. The reason is that through emotional suffering man touches the spring which opens the golden gate of his spirit and then the long grand adventure of climbing up the mountain begins.'

'I suppose the path is very lonely, White Eagle?' I said.

'No, my child, not all the time. There are places on this mountain path at which you can be joined by the true companions of your spirit. When you are able to recognise them on earth, it brings to you heaven itself - like the weary traveller coming across an oasis in the desert. But as the soul journeys

*on there are places of great beauty at which it rests and is able
to live for quite a long while.'*

*'When we had climbed some distance up the mountain I began
to see what he meant. Looking back along the path we had
travelled, the resting places changed to scenes on earth and I
saw lives which I had lived. Some, when I had given healing,
love, beauty and happiness to the world, were blessed by love
and human companionship. But I noticed also that there were
some dark and sunless spots on that path which gave no joy to
life. In other words I saw lives which had been utterly selfish
and dark.*

*White Eagle read my thoughts. 'Yes' he said, 'it is a pity, isn't
it, that people should miss so much happiness through self-will
and selfish pursuits?'...*

For anybody who would like to know more about the many
methods of communicating with the higher realms a book called
THE NEW MEDIUMSHIP, written by Grace Cooke, is essential reading and thoroughly recommended.

12

THE ANCIENT WISDOM

Men stumble over the truth from time to time but most pick
themselves up and hurry off as if nothing happened.
Sir Winston Churchill

Every major religion has evolved from the great truths of the *Ancient Wisdom.* It is said that in the golden age, at the dawn of time, certain highly evolved souls or wise ones came to this earth. They lived, taught and laboured with man bestowing their light and wisdom on what was, at that time, a receptive race. Later when the great descent (or fall) of man happened and he sank into the depths of materialism, divine laws were broken and cruelty, sin and suffering resulted. The story, in Genesis, of Adam and Eve symbolises mankind.

With the rising tide of materialism the *wise ones* retreated to the far places of the earth or to planes of existence unknown to us. However, mankind was not forsaken and periodically, in one age or another, one of them came as a teacher or saviour to offer guidance to errant mankind. These sainted ones died, often in appalling circumstances, but their message was sufficient to prevent man from completely destroying himself as a result of warlike or selfish behaviour.

Teachers appropriate to the period and race appeared - sometimes with a world wide message such as Buddha or Jesus Christ. Others came as sages or philosophers, poets, humanists, etc - but all bearing the same essential message. Unfortunately, with the passage of time, various priests have distorted the teachings and, in this connection, the Christian message is one that seems to have been somewhat tainted over the years.

Present day Christianity seems unable to answer the problems of suffering, injustice, cruelty, disease or death. It affirms that each man comes into existence at birth and, provided he toes the line, will pass onward to a splendid reward at death. In the meantime there is no logic - disease can overwhelm one's nearest and dearest, the innocent suffer and oppressors triumph. Merit goes unrewarded, wickedness is unpunished. God, the religion teaches, is a God of love and believers must simply have faith in trying circumstances.

Now the Christianity practised by Jesus of Nazareth was of a different order. Possibly one of the greatest of the *wise ones* appearing in earthly guise? His birth, youth, manhood, temptation, mission, agony at Gethsemane, trial and crucifixion, resurrection and ascension is the most powerful parable the world has seen. He was a living example of the *ancient wisdom*. For those who are familiar with these great truths it is possible to read into the Four Gospels one of the clearest and most penetrating expositions of the *ancient wisdom* man has known.

So what is this wisdom? How can it make life rational? For those hard-headed, ultra scientific, closed-minded individuals it probably will not change anything. Such individuals will want to continue to believe that life is the result of a lightning flash in a puddle (never mind where the lightning came from!) and of our gradual evolution from some primordial swamp. But, to those who are spiritually evolved, operating with the deeper intelligence of the *mind of the heart,* it is a different matter.

Orthodoxy makes the fundamental error of presenting each human life-span as a complete and separate existence with the soul commencing at birth and ending with earthly death. One might as well take one cog out of an intricate machine and then declare that the cog is the whole object. It makes little sense. The *ancient wisdom* declares life as a continuous process. If man were to live but one life here on earth it would be a sorry waste of opportunity and very uneconomic. A most un-Godlike way of carrying on! This world offers a vast field of experience for the soul of man. An infinite variety of lives. One can be born black, brown, copper, white or yellow, rich or poor, powerful or oppressed; healthy or sick. What opportunities for learning!

Of course man does not lead one life. God never wastes. Is it not reasonable to suppose that each soul must master earth's lessons before graduating elsewhere - albeit with a period of rest and recuperation between each incarnation? How little we absorb in one life-span. How much resistance do we put up to learning even the simplest lesson. The souls we meet and love in one incarnation, or life-episode, we have met and loved before. Those who wrong us must pay their debt to us and equally those whom we wrong we must repay - until hate is replaced by forgiving love. No item goes unrecorded, no wholly innocent person suffers, no cruelty stays unpunished. This is the law. The law is inexorable and undeviating. There is no imperfection. For all that there is love and there is mercy. It is through love and mercy that God redeems man and man can, in turn, redeem himself.

Without knowledge of such truths it is no small wonder that an immature soul suffering, at what he considers to be the hand of fate, under endless difficulties and hardships denies and rejects reincarnation . *One life is more than enough! I'd never come back again* he declares. No soul returns to an earthly existence except by choice. But why does anybody choose to come back? I suggest that the vision from the other side of the fence is different. The soul learns that joy, ease and refreshment palls after the sight of something which transcends all of these. The soul realises that to progress it is necessary for it to right the wrongs it has committed on earth, to fulfil those things omitted, to forgive those who have wronged it. Earthly faults and shortcomings need to be rectified - probably in the same circumstances of duress and temptation which applied when they were committed.

The soul, or the higher self, once freed from its physical limitations recognises much that was overlooked or done without due thought during testing moments on earth. It realises its failings and judges itself. Judgement, with which so many have been *threatened* comes from ourselves. With cleansed vision the soul realises that the joy and sorrow it has experienced, health or disease and all earthly events were educational processes. Such experiences produce unfoldment, development and spiritual growth. Every experience for good or ill is the logical and natural outcome of the events that preceded it.

The soul, from its higher vantage point, recognises the path ahead as an opportunity for growth. It volunteers for yet another course of experience, education and discipline which we know as physical life. The soul may select suffering or happiness, health or disease, poverty or wealth. Rather than selecting immediate ease, plenty and pleasure, the soul may take a longer view bearing in mind that each successive life is the logical outcome of that which preceded it.

The message of the *Ancients* is that all life is connected. We move in an out of incarnation gathering experience. In the process we need to learn to love one another unconditionally. We have free-will and move at the pace we choose. There is an inexorable justice and we reap as we sow. As we evolve that light within us grows brighter and the way becomes clear. We are *en route* back to the Godhead.

13

Vibrations, Chakras and Subtle Bodies

*We must disabuse our minds of the idea that these centres are
physical things. They are whirlpools of force that swirl etheric,
astral and mental matter into activity of some kind.*
Alice Bailey

I will do my best to explain the subjects covered in the next four
chapters as simply as I am able to do so. However, please bear
in mind that they cover difficult areas and esoteric terms such
as *soul, ego, higher self, celestial body, chakras, etheric, astral
and mental planes* and so on are used to mean different things
by different *authorities*. I can only explain my understanding of
them and express the hope that the broad picture will be
comprehensible to the reader. As we continue to evolve I dare
say our understanding of these matters will be clarified. In the
meantime don't worry if the next few chapters seem a bit hard
going!

All matter is vibration. Water is a liquid. We can hold it in a glass
in front of us and look at it. We can see it, touch it and sometimes
we can even smell it. If heat is applied to that water its vibration
is speeded up and it turns into steam. By cooling water its
vibration can be slowed down and it turns into solid ice. Ice,

steam and water all consist of the same components but as the vibration is speeded up or is slowed down the components assume a different state. The rate of vibration of the molecules of hydrogen oxide, which comprise water, is the sole differentiating factor. Ice the solid, water the liquid and steam the vapour are all independent of one another at the physical level and yet they are still one and the same thing. They are differentiated by their rate of molecular vibration.

The whole of the universe is based on the principle that everything is a vibration. You may recollect that the Master Jesus said that everything is light and light is, of course, a vibration. Light is a rate of molecular vibration which, in its highest form, we are unable to perceive.

Whilst we are incarnate here on earth we rely on the five senses of feeling, touch, sight, hearing and taste. These are really quite restricted. Animals and birds and various other sentient beings have more acute senses of seeing, hearing, touch and so on. We cannot see X-rays but we know they exist because we are able to see the evidence on X-ray pictures. We cannot feel them, touch them, hear them or smell them but we do not deny their existence because of this. Like the ice, water and steam it is the different speed of vibration that distinguishes one physical state from another.

What we think of as a solid block of metal is actually a construction of innumerable points of force each interlocking with the others - molecules, atoms, molecular and atomic bonds, crystalline structures and so on. Obviously it is convenient to think of items as being solid for everyday purposes. But when we leave the physical world behind us, along with our physical body, to live in the non-physical world beyond we enter a world of mind and emotions. We will be living in a world constructed from the material of thought. Thought is energy. To help illustrate the power of the mind think for a moment about dreaming, where everything appears so real but in the physical sense we have not moved from our bedroom or sleeping state.

It is important to understand that we humans are not simply a physical body. A *spirit living on earth as a human being* obviously has a *physical* body but, in addition, exists simultaneously in three other bodies namely the *etheric, astral and mental dimensions.* Over the course of time our *bodies* and *souls* incarnate into and out of these planes of existence through a process we call being *born and dying.*

The organism through which man contacts his *higher self* or *soul* is the etheric body. The *etheric* body is an exact replica of the physical body but composed of finer substance. It is a *duality* having a *lower* and *higher* part for want of better terminology. It interpenetrates the physical body and is closely connected with the nervous system. Without the *lower* or *dense etheric body* mortals would have no connection with the soul or with other worlds. It is the *bridge* which enables man to contact after-death states and the higher worlds - *a bridge between the physical and the spirit life.* All physical senses have their etheric counterpart. With the etheric counterpart of our sight, hearing, sense of smell, taste and touch we may be aware of beautiful forms that live on those *higher planes.* The etheric is closely related to the nervous system. It is this *subtle body* which registers all pleasurable sensations and, for that matter, disagreeable ones too.

At each point in the physical body, near where the ductless glands are situated, there is a corresponding *centre or vortex of nervous or psychic force in the etheric body.* Such a centre is known as a *chakra. The seven main chakras* (invisible to ordinary eyesight) are located in front of the physical spine. In ascending order, from the base of the spine to the crown of the head, these seven major energy centres are known as: *the base, sacral, solar plexus, heart, throat, brow and crown centres.* The colours are *red, orange, yellow, green, blue, indigo and violet* respectively working from the base to the crown and this assumes the chakras are functioning correctly.

The physical body is closely linked to the etheric body and it is via the chakras that the physical body gains an inflow of life force. (Conversely it is worth noting that a severe injury or shock to the physical nervous system can drive out the soul consciousness. This can also happen under the influence of excess alcohol, drugs or anaesthetic and until contact between soul and body is resumed the body remains unconscious).

The *astral body* registers the same emotions or feelings which permeate the physical body It seems that we live a lot of our earthly life in the *etheric* and *astral* bodies. Thus we feel pain or pleasure, love or hate, fear and hope - sensations and feelings of all kinds. However we must remember that the physical body is only clothing, an overcoat and when this is laid aside man continues to live on in his *subtler bodies.* The astral body is the one usually seen by clairvoyants. Its quality depends on the evolutionary state of an individual and the colours seen clairvoyantly will reflect this. As the individual evolves there is an understanding of the reality of the spiritual life and the purpose of its incarnation. Then the astral body will grow finer and the colours become more beautiful. The permanence of the *aura* (the *etheric/astral/mental dimension* visible to those individuals with *developed vision)* depends on the steady maintenance of spiritual aspirations and of gentle and refined tastes. The astral body of the ordinary person can range from dull murky colours, misty and indefinite, to a very beautiful, well formed aura, egg-like in shape, composed of definite and harmonious colours.

People who are physically *dead* but communicating with others on earth (see chapters 23, 24 and 25) are doing so from the *astral plane.* There are *lower and higher astral realms* and the level to which we ascend immediately after death depends on our state of evolvement. At that level of consciousness things are quite s*olid in appearance and feel.* But we also have to realise that what appears solid there is not immutable. *Everything can be changed by thought alone.* This means that an individual in that realm, simply by thinking of an earlier earthly body, can change his or her appearance suitably so that people from an earlier life can recognise them again.

The design of the *astral world is created by directing the subtle material of emotion and thought into forms* needed to make the individuals there feel at home, just as they felt at home in the physical world. However, because of the ease of manipulation of the subtle material on that plane, compared to physical materials, the appearance may be changed more readily than it can be changed on earth. The appearance of the surroundings is upheld for whatever purpose so long as it is needed. It can be changed by common consent. While it is upheld *that world would appear just as solid to the inhabitants on the appropriate astral plane as the earth world appears to us in our physical bodies.* When change is needed, the thought is changed for the required purpose. The material again becomes fluid to re-form into the apparently quite solid shapes required.

This process can, in fact, take place at the physical level with physical materials. Most people have heard of the spoon benders! Physical materials too, can soften, bend and solidify under the action of strongly directed forces of thought. Science, as yet, has no answer to this except fraud and hocus pocus which, with the evidence presented, is scarcely an adequate explanation!

Of finer vibration, but interpenetrating the other subtle bodies, is the egg shaped form of the *aura of the mental body*. It can change rapidly with changing thoughts. There is a *higher and lower mental body*. The *lower mental deals with intellectual matters* and the *higher mental with spiritual things*. The mental plane comes closer to the *higher self which is sometimes called the angelic or heavenly body*. We are told it is most beautiful in appearance and shining with a great light. Every human being has such a body at a certain stage of development. This *higher self* for which I think we can also read *soul* has evolved during many, many lives and is, in reality, the *temple of man's spirit* in the *celestial realms*. This is the plane of the angelic hierarchies, the saints and perfected souls of all ages. Such souls would have passed through great tribulations in this world and through their experiences in countless incarnations have evolved to become harmonised with the divine law of love.

The *soul* is the *individuality* but not the personality. What we know as the *personality is the outer self* - not the soul. The *personality is not the real individual* but an aspect which manifests on the earth plane today. *The personality represents only a small part of that greater soul* which lives in a higher state of consciousness. For all that the personality is in touch, to a greater or lesser extent, with that greater soul of higher consciousness. The amount of contact between the earthly personality and the higher self will depend, I suggest, on the degree of evolvement of the individual. In some cases the personality might be able to draw from it at will.

The soul is not the spirit. The spirit has been described as: *the divine spark, that which fires the engine - the spark igniting the propulsive force, the spirit which is fire, which is purity, which is the very essence of God in man.* The spirit is the perfect directing energy that marks out the path of the soul through its various incarnations. As we evolve, work and strive on the earth plane in succeeding incarnations we are building our *celestial body* (home of the soul in my understanding) which is *parked* on a particular plane of consciousness. This *parking place* is established as a result of its many physical experiences - not necessarily on the earth planet by the way! Our *parking spot* is dependent on our overall degree of evolvement.

When a person dies a form arises and passes out and away through the head of the dying body. This is the *lower or denser etheric body* and would be visible to a clairvoyant person. It appears as a vapoury mass which gradually consolidates and forms a body which is an exact replica of the physical. Encased in it, or permeating the *denser etheric body,* is the *higher etheric body* composed of different grades of white ether. It is that *subtler part of man* which we call the *soul.* It is the *higher self,* the invisible clothing of the spirit. The soul has been built upon ever since the spirit was *breathed forth* from God.

Soon after physical death the *soul or higher self* separates from the *lower etheric* and ascends to a higher state of consciousness - to the particular astral plane prepared for it. The *etheric double* of the physical body disintegrates in due course as does the physical body. *The soul remains - it is the store-house of all the experiences of the past.* Within it is held the memory of man's past lives on earth and elsewhere. It holds the experiences and memories of the soul's own past coupled with information acquired during visits to higher worlds and in higher planes of living.

By the way it sometimes happens that the *lower etheric body* does not always disintegrate immediately after physical death. It has been known to linger about places familiar to the deceased individual. When this happens the etheric emanation left behind is not the true self although it can survive for quite a long time, keeping close to the earth. This is what we know as a *wraith or ghost.*

As suggested earlier the home of the soul is the *celestial body.* It is the highest and most pure aspect. This is the *temple of the spirit - our permanent body in the heavens.* It is to this *celestial body* that the individual finally withdraws after passing through the experiences of the earth, the astral dimension, the *Summerland* (the realm we normally go to soon after death) and the mental life. The *celestial body,* through its contact with the earth, absorbs certain lessons which are retained to be used in future states, either in or out of incarnation. Only that which is useful is retained and it is known as the permanent or seed atom. This permanent atom provides for the creation of the vehicles we shall inhabit during our next incarnation. Thus the *celestial body* is built by our actions and reactions, by our thoughts and desires. We are told that the aura of a beautiful *celestial body* consists of colours almost impossible to describe in earthly terms.

We create substance out of the higher ethers which will, in the fullness of time, manifest once more on the earth plane when we reincarnate (see chapter 14). Thus we create our physical vehicles - our own present physical body. When living in that higher state, *in the celestial condition,* from which we descend to reincarnate, we realise the need for certain material. The individual becomes dissatisfied with his *particular temple of the spirit* or *celestial body* and realises that the only way to find more and better material is to return to physical life and earn the new conditions. The old soul, after a better *parking place* in the celestial realms, reincarnates in a physical body to gather more experience.

14

REINCARNATION

A little while, a moment of rest upon the wind and another woman shall bear me.
Kahlil Gibran

The primary fact of historical existence is that all things, both living and inanimate, come into being and later vanish. This is true on every scale. The galactic system itself has not always existed. It was born billions of years ago and at some point in the future it will die. During the time our universe has been in existence it has gradually produced the sun, the earth, and an environment capable of supporting life as we know it. It gave birth to the human race a relatively short time ago - a few million years at most. During that time billions of individual human beings have lived and died. We have collectively evolved a civilisation capable of landing man on the moon or killing thousands of people at a stroke.

What governs this process of birth and death, of growth and development? Scientists tend to rely on the various theories of evolution in their search for these answers but a scientific approach has limitations. The main problem is that scientific theories of evolution deal only with the physical dimension, which is only one aspect of a much more complicated reality. When, and if, these theories are ever proven they are inherently incapable of explaining anything beyond the facts of physical development. What of the much larger question of the evolution of the human mind and the human spirit? For answers to this we have to look to mystics rather than scientists.

I suggest that it is important to understand that we are eternal and central to that understanding is the concept of reincarnation. Reincarnation is part of the philosophy of the *ancient wisdom,* already discussed in chapter 12, and is a natural consequence of *karma* (see next chapter). As indicated earlier we need to see life as an eternal process. Our biggest mistake is thinking that the *real life* is the physical world we are experiencing now. The continuing stream of life is really *on the other side* where we go when we *die.* This is punctuated by episodes of existence in many earth lives where we learn from our experiences.

The *real life,* which is to say the life in spirit, coupled with periodic descents into the physical world, or reincarnation, has been likened to school term and holidays. During the term at school, or incarnation, life is enjoyable on occasion but mostly it is hard work and sometimes it is very uncomfortable. That is when we learn a lot. When term ends we go on *holiday,* via physical death, and rest for a while before returning for another term of learning.

In the life between earth lives, called *the bardo* by some, it is not necessary to extend oneself or make any great effort. We can take it very easy if we like but there are opportunities to extend ourselves if we wish to do so. The periods on earth, which are far from easy for most people, are to give us the difficult experiences we need to balance the equation. However, in the spiritual sense, we can speed our evolvement by taking the opportunity to learn whilst we are on holiday. The choice is ours. We also choose, with a lot of help from more evolved individuals, the circumstances of our earthly incarnations with a view to learning something at a soul level. Of the many books on this subject one that I found of particular interest is called LIFE BETWEEN LIFE by a Dr. Whitton and a reporter called Joe Fisher.

The hypothesis that we are persuaded to return to earth, again and again, in different bodily vehicles is well supported by cultural tradition, religious doctrine and countless personal experiences or recollections. Acceptance of rebirth goes hand in hand with exploration of our true spiritual natures. Rebirth has always been espoused by the wisest of spiritual and philosophical sages from Plato to the Master Jesus. Tribal memory, ancient myth and fable, religious belief and classical wisdom all bear witness to the conviction that repeated incarnations are as essential for spiritual evolution as the succession of years is to physical development. Rebirth has always been seen as the framework of immortality or the means by which perfect enlightenment can, eventually, be attained.

Over a billion Asiatics, thanks to Hindu and Buddhist teachings, accept that they must undergo round after round of birth and death in their pursuit of knowledge. They aspire to deliverance from the *wheel of rebirth* by leading lives of selflessness and compassion. The ancient Greeks and Egyptians had a sophisticated awareness of the process of reincarnation. The ancient inhabitants of northern Europe were so sure of rebirth that they wept in commiseration at the birth of a child and greeted death with rejoicing. The Druids, with even greater conviction, were supposed to have accepted that if borrowed money could not be repaid in this life, the debt could be made good in the next incarnation.

Child prodigies provide some evidence for the view that talent is not necessarily developed in one remarkable life but is more likely to have it's origins in previous physical existence's.

Even though orthodox Christianity, Judaism and Islam presently deny reincarnation, members of each of these great schools of religious thought have argued the case for it. Rebirth was widely accepted by many early Christians, notably by Origen who, with the possible exception of Emperor Augustine, was one of the most prominent of the church patrons. At the Council of Constantinople (see chapter 9) it was the Emperor Justinian who put his foot down about reincarnation. This censure was followed by persecution of everybody who refused to think the same way. Resistance was considerable, especially by rebel Christians called the Cathars and it was not until the thirteenth century that the church's campaign of terror and slaughter effectively silenced such thinking in the West.

In different cultures there are different ideas concerning the nature of the soul's return into physical existence. Some people believe, for instance, that the return is not necessarily in human form but that one can be in the body of, say, an animal. Other teachings state that having an individual soul differentiates humans from the animal kingdom. Unlike animals, humans have an awakening consciousness of the divine. This progress cannot be reversed and, on this basis, it is impossible for a human soul to reincarnate in an animal form. The human soul has free-will as to how it will react to people and circumstances. Animals, on the other hand, come under the care and direction of a group spirit who gives them their innate instincts for survival and growth. A group spirit will direct the migration of birds or the habits of each particular species.

The same teaching states that animals eventually attain to the human level of evolution through association with the humans they serve. Love between the two can grow, perhaps over a number of lives, till it reaches the point where the animal friend is so full of devotion that it will sacrifice it's life for the beloved master or mistress. The growth of love in the animal soul gradually brings such an attachment to the human life that it withdraws from the group and starts on the human path towards individualisation. This surely demonstrates the immense importance of treating animals with love and respect especially those who have reached the stage of their evolution of being drawn to human companionship. Such animals even sacrifice their bodies in the service of their human guardians. This service is part of the great lesson of love which gradually brings the soul, whether human or animal, a deeper understanding.

In the human state it seems that the young soul is, at first, drawn into a closely-knit human group, family or tribe. Here again, it is completely obedient to the leader and to the customs of the group. Gradually, through many lives, the mind develops independence, bringing an urge for individualisation. This leads progressively to the time when, instead of blindly following the animal instincts of the body, the soul desires to understand more of the *whence, whither* and *why* of existence. Thus, gradually, the soul evolves from the animal to the human and from the human to the divine - to full consciousness of the Creator.

Some people get rather vexed when offered biblical explanations, fables and fairy tales in connection with our history. However, in destroying these myths the baby is often thrown out with the bath water. There is usually a deep truth in the story but the original meaning may be lost. For example, what about Adam and Eve in the Garden of Eden? In this tale man once dwelt in a home of peace and plenty, of joy and happiness, innocent children of God with no knowledge of what lay outside Eden. But having once tasted the fruits of the Tree of Knowledge, Adam and Eve realised that there was much to learn. It was their choice to taste that fruit and so they went out from the Garden. With their new found knowledge it had ceased to be heaven for them. Spiritually they were aware that they needed to leave the Garden of Eden to gain experience and to use the knowledge they would gain.

The myth describes how Adam and Eve were obliged to leave heaven, which is to say leave the home of God their father, in order to incarnate into the physical world. In that world they had to earn their *bread* to feed not only their bodies but also their minds, souls and spirits. Humankind has been on that journey ever since, gaining experience and learning through joy and sorrow, pleasure and pain, success and failure. Adam and Eve were not allowed to return to the Garden of Eden until they could get past the angel guarding the gate. To get past that angel they needed a password consisting of a number of letters. Every lesson perfectly learned amounts to a letter of the password and, like Adam and Eve, we can return to the heaven world when we have finally had sufficient experience in our many, many lives.

From the beginning of time the group or family consciousness is part of the soul's growth. It seems that souls continue to work through many lives with their family group. This does not necessarily mean the blood family but a group of souls who can work together harmoniously to help one another's evolution. When a soul reincarnates it does so with a certain mission to learn. We may find ourselves loving and working with those whom we have loved and helped as well as those whom we have injured or hated. The eventual object being to forgive and make good all the hurts, to *straighten all the crooked places,* and to transform all hate and dissension into brotherly love and understanding.

Prior to incarnation and before physical conception the soul makes contact with the body of the potential mother. It gradually merges itself into the physical body as the years advance. By the age of about 21 the soul has generally incarnated in full but this is an approximation as it appears there is no precise or finite period which applies to everybody.

Simply stated, reincarnation means the periodic descent of the soul to labour in this world. Creation is governed by the supreme principles of love and wisdom. Thus, having spent a lifetime on planet Earth (which, in retrospect, may seem about as long as the blinking of an eye) the soul withdraws from earthly activity to rejoin its true self. It returns to its real home in the heaven world for rest and refreshment and in order to assimilate the lessons it has learned.

For many, reincarnation answers all the problems concerning the inequality of man's lot in his present life. They are content to know that what they meet in this life, for either good or ill, is the result of their past actions. The question often arises about why we cannot remember our past lives. Such memories are stored in the higher self of man and until sufficient spiritual development is obtained, or until the soul is ready to face these memories, it is impossible for the brain to receive impressions from that higher memory.

Before coming into incarnation again there is that period of peace and quiescence, of rest and recuperation. When we shed our physical body at the end of a particular incarnation the soul sees a picture of its whole journey so far. The decision is then made as to what further experience and growth is needed. That is where the real free-will is manifest. The soul may, perhaps, choose an easy life or it may be given such a vision of the ultimate perfection that it longs to clear its debts quickly, so that it may become one with that heavenly beauty and peace. In this case it may choose a very difficult incarnation, perhaps with a severely handicapped body or mind, or one in which there is almost unbearable emotional strain and suffering.

When we are in the presence of men and women and children whose minds are disturbed we may well wonder how anybody, who does not know where they are or what day it is, can learn anything about the love of God or how they might progress spiritually. How can they grow when they have no comprehension? It is difficult to know how such individuals learn anything in such circumstances but the evidence is that nothing happens by chance. Everything is the outworking of a divine and loving plan. For our part we cannot judge by the outward manifestation and need to remember that there is an inner life

At the etheric and soul level, whatever the outward disabilities, that soul may well be active in the inner world close to the earth - perhaps even helping others in need - thanks to their own disability giving them increased understanding of those afflicted individuals. It is also worth bearing in mind that it is only a facet of the jewel that comes back into incarnation at any one time. Sometimes we choose to come back to the earth in a handicapped body or with a handicapped mind because in our higher selves we know that this is the way we can learn a deep and important soul lesson that, possibly, we could not learn in any other way. We also have to take into account the opportunities given to those around the individuals for karmic outworking and soul lessons through service and compassion. We can certainly learn lessons even if we have no comprehension with our *little everyday mind* about what is going on.

It has long been recognised that the first seven years of life are vital in the formation of character. When we understand the truth of reincarnation and karma we realise that character, although shaped by our parents and the family environment, has been developed through our habitual thoughts and actions in past lives. The soul is drawn to those parents with whom it has some deep emotional link from the past, either positive or negative. *The genes of those parents will give the required body and their auras will supply the necessary soul environment for further progress on the path of evolution.* In the same way parents draw to themselves souls whose karma is interlinked with their own. They will be able to help those souls as well as learning from them.

Every soul is born under the care and direction of a guardian angel. The guardian angel ensures that the individual comes into incarnation at the moment when its first breath enables it to draw in appropriate planetary vibrations to form the blueprint of that life. We learn so much through the experiences of the physical body - its strength or weakness, its perfection's or imperfections and its health or disharmony. As the soul develops and unfolds, memories of the past start to awaken and it begins to recognise exactly why it is faced with certain conditions in the present life.

The soul will accept what is happening, knowing that the law is just, perfect and true. The soul also knows that by its reaction to any adversity in the present-day life it will create new opportunities for the future. Many people are already in touch, in some measure, with their past lives and that can sometimes help them to come to terms with their current difficulties.

Reincarnation is a metaphysical proposition, like the concept of heaven and hell. It cannot be measured scientifically or judged by our earthly limitations. Proof must give way to perception. One has to know it is so from within. However, all the eloquence and evidence in the world will not make the idea any more palatable to the individual who chooses to believe otherwise.

15

KARMA

We choose our joys and sorrows long before we experience them.
Kahlil Gibran

The modern world appears confused and beset with problems. Scientific and technical knowledge is gradually destroying both superstition and conventional religion. It is also depriving many of the faith which sustained their fathers. Unfortunately, it offers nothing in its place - no guiding star for which many people unconsciously long. More and more young people with highly trained minds find that the orthodox religious beliefs seem unreasonable and provide no answer to human problems. Such problems have always existed but are now made more complex by the increasing speed and freedom of modern life and the problems facing the planet on all fronts.

Humans lie, steal and betray one another. In fact they do everything that the Ten Commandments forbid. Why is this the normal pattern? When man was given material form he was also given free-will. Some chose to do good and the remainder otherwise. This is the way that humans learn and grow. We reap as we sow. Cause and effect. Our experiences on earth make this clear but it seems to take most of us a long time to appreciate the fact. It is hard to acknowledge that we have only ourselves to blame for our experiences.

Karma, as it is called in the East, is that which individuals have set in motion for themselves from lifetime to lifetime by their motivations, attitudes and behaviour. Acceptance of karma dismisses the idea that humans are mere pawns in a cosmic chess game. To accept karma is to acknowledge that the world is an arena of natural justice. There can be no unfairness, inequality and misfortune if all conditions arise as a direct result of past conduct. Karma links self-responsibility to the law of cause and effect. One's actions from life to life give shape and substance to personal continuity and personal destiny. Buddha put it succinctly, but enigmatically, when he said: *If you want to know the past look at your present life. If you want to know the future look at your present.*

Every action causes a reaction. Both positive and negative circumstances are caused by karma. Our personalities are the result of cumulative karma. We are what we have experienced and how we deal with what we have learned. Momentum is essential to personal evolution. Without momentum there would be no learning, there would be nothing to propel the soul through the many experiences that arise in the course of its journeying from incarnation to incarnation.

Traditionally defined, karma is a system of retributive justice that perpetuates rebirth and determines the form and setting of each succeeding incarnation. The ancients taught that karma is discharged according to *an eye for an eye* philosophy. This maintains that, sooner or later, people will experience for themselves precisely the joys and sorrows they have created for others. However, it does not have to work out exactly that way because we have the opportunity to transmute the karmic consequences of earlier activity by serving our fellow men. When we help another we help ourselves.

Karmic debts can be transmuted in various ways. To recognise a past mistake is half the battle. Once aware of an error it is a natural impulse to want to do something to recompense the person one has wronged. If one is aware of having behaved badly in the past then by giving service to the aggrieved person or persons the slate can be wiped clean so far as a particular incident is concerned.

How many times do we see events in our daily lives which are apparently inexplicable? An *innocent* person suffers and a *rogue* escapes punishment. A child dies and a dictator lives. When we understand karma we realise that we can judge no individual. It is the law that rules the countless incarnations of the soul. We cannot sow thistles and reap roses

Perhaps the invention of the computer with its built-in memory, makes it easier for us to comprehend the precise and inexorable law of karma. We are re-born always into an environment where we meet again those we have wronged or by whom we have been wronged. Equally we meet again those whom we have helped or who have helped us, as well as those to whom we are linked by a bond of deep love. This is particularly true of family relationships.

It is worth remembering that through the experience of many incarnations a soul will incur certain karmic debts. These karmic debts cannot be paid off until sufficient wisdom and strength has been gained to enable an individual to deal with them. Some spiritual sources teach that no soul returns to earth with a heavier load than it can bear. Nonetheless, I dare say we have all wondered about that, from time to time, when life has been particularly testing!

So called *bad karma* is created not only by lack of love but by absence of wisdom, by ignorance. Until a soul experiences for itself it cannot know, or understand, or appreciate what love is. Through experience the soul acquires love and wisdom. However when it comes to the question of ignorance we are sailing in tricky waters. I take the view that man is not so ignorant as not to know that selfishness and greed are wrong, yet he frequently persists in them and, in so doing, brings suffering upon himself. There is a difference between innocent ignorance and wilful ignorance. In the latter case one really knows, deep down, that there is a denial of that inner voice or conscience.

The world is a miraculous place. One is continually struck by the fact that everything arises out of nothingness. Every existence, even an existence that appears bad or evil, needs to be treasured. In the journey of waves across the ocean we see a continual change between highness and lowness. We don't call the high good and the low bad but recognise that if the low places did not exist as a base then the high places could not exist either. The summit of a mountain could not exist without the base. The whole is composed of it's parts. We would not understand joy if we did not know sorrow. When one comes to understand karma for what it is, one realises the inherent inter-connectedness of all beings.

Karma is the law of cause and effect and linked with this is the law of opportunity. It must not be thought of as something bad or as a punishment for transgressions in the past. It is more an opportunity to balance the books. On its long journey the soul receives continual opportunity to attain divine illumination.

Good fortune such as winning the lottery, premium bonds or holiday trip, etc, may equally be karmic and a recognition of some kind deed of long ago. On the other hand it may also be a test to see how we cope with responsibility! During every incarnation lessons are presented, or tests if you prefer, which are actually opportunities for progress and initiation.

16

CREATION AND THE CHRIST LIGHT VEHICLE

In the centre of everything is the sun.
Nicholas Copernicus

When the human mind tries to comprehend the meaning of the universe it usually gives up. It is impossible for us, with our limited understanding, to know the reason for it all. I have already touched on the *whence, whither and why* of our existence and we can, perhaps, understand that there is an energy behind everything. For convenience we can call that energy God or the Creator.

In ancient days when men were spiritually quickened they possessed knowledge, passed to them by their teachers, of a spiritual power or directing influence behind their lives. This found expression for them in the form of the physical sun. They actually worshipped the sun. They knew that the sun not only gave them life and warmth but also spirit. They realised that behind the physical form which they saw in the heavens was a spiritual radiation, the spiritual life force upon which their life depended.

Life in every form is created and sustained from the sun. The sun is the heart of the solar system and from the sun there shines a spiritual radiance. What we experience on earth as heat and light is but a reflection of that radiance of the spiritual sun. In the same way, the heart in our own physical body is the life giver and the power which motivates it. There is an aura or radiance around our physical bodies with the heart at its centre. We are miniature solar systems. On a smaller scale the very cells in our body have their nucleus or centre radiating energy. Moving to the other end of the scale we have only to glance at the sky on a clear night to get some idea what a small part of the universe our little galaxy represents.

Here are two quotations. The first is from a scientific source and is as follows: *Life is itself a manifestation of light. Light starts up life, governs growth and stimulates behaviour.* The second quotation is from dear old White Eagle: *Without the spiritual light no earthly life would exist. You are only alive because of this golden sunlight behind the sun. You are cold and dead without this renewing life.*

In Biblical terms we are told: *In the beginning was the Word and the Word was with God and the Word was God.* God, this Father/Mother energy said: *Let there be Light. Light,* then, was the first creation of God, or put another way, the *First-Born or Son of God. The First-Born* is the *Light,* or *Christ,* or *Cosmic Christ* as it is called in some esoteric teachings. It is the spiritual counterpart of the physical sun of our solar system.

When we hear the words: *Christ, the First-Born, the Only Begotten Son,* the words refer to the manifestation of the *Light* created by the *Parent-of-All* who is both male and female energy, combined in perfect balance. This is important to understand for in *separation,* or *descent,* into a three dimensional world, the Creator's wholeness suffered division into *duality* on earth. Here we have become denser or solidified into the separate parts that we call male and female.

The Creator despatched souls as *sparks of light enshrined within a dense physical overcoat,* to experience the evolutionary process of descending into physical matter. The light, continuing to shine as a beacon in the darkness and during the evolutionary process, gradually growing brighter. When we *return to God* and lose the density of the physical body we become a form of light containing both male and female principles in balanced proportion.

The physical body of the male when compared with the female is not much different although there are, of course, differences in the reproductive organs. However, the female reproductive organs have only to be externalised to turn her into a male. Sexual differentiation itself is not that important and whether we are a man or woman is really no big deal. Our mental body is sexless. (One might well wonder about all the fuss over woman priests!) Sometimes we incarnate in the physical body of a man and sometimes a woman.

Among mammals, all sexual differentiation begins with the basic female patterning. Only with the introduction of a special protein which acts to create the testicles does the male of the species appear. Sex is a microcosm of the creation of all life on this planet. Unhappily mankind, with its penchant for double standards and hypocrisy, has built an industry around it and complicated the essential simplicity beyond all measure, resulting in aberrations of all sorts.

On the higher spiritual planes the bodies of male and female are alike so it is reasonable to conclude that these two opposites were only created for the convenience of incarnating spirits. Man and woman only identify themselves as opposites in order to make themselves responsible for new life seeking admission to the physical world. The immaculate conception has a mystical meaning as well as its more commonly understood sense. The solar logos or great spirit behind the sun drew together atoms and created form under the command of the Creator. Thus life on the planet earth began.

There is a great deal of confusion between Jesus of Nazareth and the *First Born,* sometimes called the *Light* or the *Christ.* It is important to understand that those latter names apply to the *Only Begotten Son* and not the Master Jesus - although He became known as the *Christ* because He was such a great channel for the *Light.* There is a distinction between Jesus and the *First Born,* otherwise known as the *Light* or *Christ.* Jesus is, like the rest of us, a child of God but He, above all, was a *supreme channel for that Light.* The *Christ Light* is, of course, not limited to Him alone but shines, at least in some measure, in all our hearts.

The First Born, Cosmic Christ or Being of Light or Christ Light has an aura which permeates more than earth. The vibrations of this aura reach to the innermost of every living person. This energy, which is the light in all beings on the planet, obviously surpasses all human comprehension.

It is, perhaps, not so difficult to understand that it was impossible for the Bearer of that Christ Light to descend and be born as an ordinary human being although it is my understanding that the conception of Jesus was immaculate. I assume this did not apply to his 4 brothers and sisters (Matthew chapter 6, verse 3). There was no vehicle to draw down this energy into incarnation

110

on earth and a Being had to be made ready for this purpose. That Being was Jesus of Nazareth. Jesus was prepared through many incarnations, not only on earth, but beginning before humanity as we understand it. He was not of this earth's lifestream, which is to say that His Being is much older than this earth. He had been through experiences of a very exalted nature in preparation for His mission - the full power of which is yet to be realised by the mass of earth people.

The Master Jesus was a pure soul who descended, step by step, from the highest source to this earth planet. In doing so he took upon himself various forms and bodies. All His incarnations were leading up to the appointed time when He would take the great incarnation which would radiate light and blessing. That heavenly light, the sun, that supreme light of the heavens the *Christ Light* simply poured through Jesus. The *Christ Light* had flowed, in some degree, through many other great Teachers through the ages. However, in Jesus of Nazareth it manifested in a greater degree than in any other Master or Teacher. The arrival of Jesus was the culmination of the Christ power which was, and is, to flood the earth and all mankind.

In his life as Jesus of Nazareth he was trained in the Brotherhood of the Essenes. The Essenes taught the unfoldment of the inner light. These Brothers served the community in simple ways, tilling the soil, weaving, doing carpentry and all manner of handicraft. They conducted themselves with great love and gentleness. They were taught always of the principles of God, of their Oneness with God, of the sacredness of the earth. They blessed the food that they ate and they had a reverence for all life. It was from this community that the Master Jesus came. He was prepared both spiritually and physically to be a physical vehicle through which the *Christ Light* could shine.

The mission of Jesus was to bring to humanity the teaching of love, because all human development and the development of the earth itself is based upon the common denominator love. The message from Jesus was very simple. *Love one another. Love is the fulfilling of the law. Love in man's heart is his saving grace.*

17

CHRISTIANITY, THE CHURCH, THE CRUCIFIXION AND THE NEW AGE

Who can separate his faith from his actions, or his belief from his occupations?
Kahlil Gibran

The established Church promises us a rather vague heaven at the end of our time on earth. This is conditional on our behaviour and applies only if we have *toed the line*. If we do not - then some religions promise us hell and damnation, or extinction, at the very least.

Intuitively we long for something better than that. Deep within us is the knowledge that we are, indeed, spiritual creatures. We need to cultivate that link with our spiritual consciousness although it is not easy in this material world. This is especially so now that scientists have the answer for everything. Or nearly everything!

As already discussed, Jesus of Nazareth had a simple lifestyle - certainly not that of a rich man. It is difficult to reconcile the life He lead with the lifestyle and ornate robes of certain high church dignitaries we see today. There is such a contrast between the messages of the parables and the curious behaviour of some influential members of the established order in this day and age.

The first definitive breach between the basic teachings and those of the Church came at the Council of Nicea in AD325 (see chapter 9) when Christianity became the new-fangled belief of the Roman Emperor Constantine. Constantine needed to re-establish the seemingly defunct Roman Empire and needed a unifying factor to inspire his people. His mother was already a Christian so when he examined the teachings of Jesus of Nazareth he felt that he had found his man.

The Council of Nicea was assembled to formalise his new religion but, by all accounts, the meeting was far from peaceful. Arius, a celebrated writer much persecuted because of his belief that God was divisible, caused a disagreement. According to Arius - God was divisible and had sent the spirit of Christ *(the Light)* to inhabit the body of Jesus of Nazareth - thus transforming him into a Holy Soul in a mortal body. In short Jesus was a human being but completely imbued by Spirit. Arius had his followers but the Council was split.

Emperor Constantine came up with his own version of what the belief should be which was that the *Father, Son and Holy Ghost* are indivisible (consubstantial in theological terms meaning of the same substance). By that he meant that those three - known as the *Trinity* are one lot and humankind another. Anybody refusing to sign up to the new dogma was excommunicated. The authorities now felt free to teach that God *(Father, Son and Holy Ghost or Trinity)* is unique and indivisible. It then became the official view of Christianity. Arius, as already stated, believed that Jesus was not only the Son of God but also an impeccable mortal, inspired by God. This belief was thus thrown out of official Christianity and Arius along with it! Since one of the main themes of this book is the oneness of all life you will understand that my own view accords with that of Arius!

In the year AD384 Jerome freely admitted that he had amended the early scriptures to bring them into line with what he thought had really happened. Thus the Holy Bible today is based on Jerome's Latin translation. The Council of Constantinople in AD553 and the rejection of reincarnation has already been discussed. I am not an expert on the history and development of the Christian Church but merely report on what I have understood in reading about it. I have mentioned some of the highlights to show that a particular truth, through the ages, can be distorted and how easy it is for a new belief to become established.

It is difficult to understand what is meant by the Church when they say that because Jesus was crucified He took the sins of humanity *upon His own shoulders.* Does this mean we can treat people as badly as we like because Jesus has already been crucified on our account? I suspect not.

As I understand it Jesus taught a simple message of love and service to one's fellow men. It is not Jesus the man, as a human being, who saves the world but, on the other hand, He is a Saviour because through Him came the message of love not only in regard to man's material life but for the development of man's spirit as well. His human life was an example of divine love. The message was not only in regard to man's material life but for the development of man's spirit as well.

Humanity associates the cross as a symbol of the sacrifice of the Nazarene Jesus but it is also an age old symbol which we all *see* at a certain stage of spiritual evolution. The symbol is found in all civilisations and in every race as an outward symbol of an inward experience. That experience is of surrender, of complete self-giving. When the blindfold is removed from the eyes of the aspiring soul it sees the light and cross of self-surrender. The cross is a symbol of life - but of life gained through death, not of the physical body but of the dense lower self. The cross symbolises the surrender of the lower nature, the relinquishing of personal desire and complete surrender to the will of God.

Why did the crucifixion have to take place? I think it is much misunderstood. In my understanding it is a symbol of spiritual growth and of the evolution of man - the symbol of the initiation of the earth. It is one of the four great initiations which every human soul must undergo on its journey back to God. Crucifixion is the earth initiation. This initiation is the highest point of man's life in a physical body. Everything that Jesus was called upon to face during His crucifixion was endured in a spirit of perfect love. We don't have to endure physical crucifixion but we would do well to emulate the Nazarene when we are tested in our daily lives. This, I believe, is the very heart of the spiritual meaning of the earth initiation.

The whole story of the crucifixion shows, as incident follows incident, the exceeding love in the heart of the Master. He clearly demonstrated that in passing through a spiritual initiation the great need was for love; for the soul to meet all trials and suffering in a spirit of loving surrender. Jesus demonstrated his great love for his fellow men by his attitude to Judas, the man who betrayed him (Matthew 10:4). Symbolically Judas represents the lower aspect of every man. We all have a Judas nature in us and it is this nature that lets us down, betraying the Christ spirit within us. We have to learn to forgive ourselves as well as others. Again, Jesus recognised in Judas one who had, in the past, himself been a victim of betrayal (Mark 13:12, Luke 21:16). Thus it was natural for Judas to betray Jesus - the instinct to do to another what had been done to him.

In it can be read the story of the liberation of the spirit from the domination of the flesh and earthly matter. It is an experience awaiting every soul on its path of evolution. Every one of us goes through some experience which might be described as crucifixion; some experience involving great pain and soul-anguish. When this happens we are, in a sense, doing something for the whole world, especially if we can meet such testing of the soul with a resolute and tranquil spirit. By so doing we are raising the vibration of the whole earth.

Now we are moving into a New Age called the Golden or Aquarian Age. It is a time of energy change and uplifting for all humanity. It is a time when the things formerly invisible can be made real to us. A time of joining heaven and earth together in open communication and co-operation. We have to change our limiting habits and recognise within ourselves our higher, or soul-selves, whilst still living in physical form. We must build a bridge of energy between the personality and soul-self to achieve this. This is the time for the alignment of the lowest and highest into one motive and one action. Love.

The major world religions of the past brought teachers to the world in physical bodies. These prophets came to share their understanding of the teachings with others. It was necessary to do it this way since most human beings had no awareness of an inner connection to Spirit. It was the only way to spread the word but, in the Golden Age, there will be a shift from this former pattern so that every soul may speak directly to it's higher self. Through the process of meditation and contemplation, in times of silence and solitude, it is possible to experience direct inner messages and obtain assistance in that way.

In this New Age we have to put away the old rugged cross of crucifixion and replace it with one of growth and understanding. When Jesus came as the *Bearer of the Light* it was necessary for Him to take on a physical body in which to reside and prove to humanity that there is no death to the true identity. Anyway Jesus is now moved on from the crucifixion. It is over and done with and we must see Jesus alive and beautiful and forget the story of crucifixion and all its guilt and pain. In place of a crucified body on a cross we can use the symbol of an equisided cross within a circle, or a rainbow or a glowing sun to denote life or growth or unity. Let us forgive ourselves for anything real or imagined related to that event 2,000 years ago. Remember how Jesus forgave Judas! The Christian religion is full of guilt and negativity and it needs to be changed.

The way in which we have all evolved over the past 2,000 years applies equally to the heaven world. Heaven is not a static place. We are related to the Universe. Each is part of the whole, from the macrocosm to the microcosm. On earth we are a hologram of the greater universal pattern. Great in wisdom and love as the Master Jesus was in the past. He is now more perfected - as are all spiritual beings who come to teach us.

18

GOOD AND EVIL

You cannot separate the just from the unjust and the good from
the wicked; For they stand together before the face of the sun
even as the black thread and the white are woven together. And
when the black thread breaks, the weaver shall look into the
whole cloth, and he shall examine the loom also.
Kahlil Gibran

All life consists of two aspects - positive and negative, light and darkness, good and evil, constructive and destructive. The one is antagonistic to the other. We react to their influences and feel attracted or repelled by them. Good and evil are like two wheels (one within the other) continually at work - the higher and the lower. The action of the lower always brings suffering but a suffering designed to produce the perfect archetype or perfected man.

It has to be recognised that the forces of good and evil both come from the Creator. Many people are unable to accept this. We must remember that the Creator is omnipotent, omniscient and omnipresent and mankind lives in this very heart. Yet there are two aspects and when these are understood and rightly viewed man can see the purpose of what is called evil.

Love of power is behind what often passes for evil. The lower aspect of man asserts itself and a desire for power rises in his mind. Thus man fell from his perfect state, tempted by what we call evil, as a result of love of power. Bear in mind, though, that this same desire also caused development and growth of the individual soul and mind. So called evil produces individualisation, a necessary part of the process of evolution. Without this pushing forward of the self, this individualisation, there would be little urge to grow towards the ideal of a completed, perfected son of God.

Evil represents the unevolved and undeveloped aspect of life and is also the consuming, the destructive force, the fire which tries man's mettle and absorbs and removes that which has become unwanted. Instead of attacking to rid the world of evil it is preferable to radiate love, light, beauty and truth.

Discrimination between the true and false, between the real and unreal, between right and wrong, between the promptings of our higher and lower selves is one of the primary lessons on the path. This cannot be taught. It has to be gained through experience and meditation. It is a tricky one. We need to look at every problem first from the spiritual aspect rather than the immediately obvious and then ponder about its meaning. We can only pray for help to get the right answer and then hope for the best.

Once incarnate in a particular life we do not really have as much free-will as we might like to imagine. The soul is placed in certain conditions in its physical life which afford it opportunities to serve the great karmic law . New circumstances arise continually and the testing is thorough. Freewill lies in the soul's response to the various opportunities presented. Ideally we take the conditions offered with loving acceptance but some-times we fail. The elder brethren oversee our efforts with love and compassion. The thought is that we have done our best and they are sorry to see us suffer.

As we become more enlightened we no longer see situations which we dislike, or where we appear to suffer, as undesirable. We realise that the laws of the Creator are perfectly just. Whatever happens in our outer life and however unpleasant it may seem to the outer mind, there will be a compensating blessing behind it.

As already indicated we cannot judge another. An individual's past history is unknown to us and we don't know why he acts as he does. There is a wonderful old Native Indian saying, summing it up nicely, which runs something like this: *Don't judge any man until you have walked two moons in his moccasins*. That's two months! The person we may be tempted to judge could be an instrument of divine law. This may be difficult to understand but it goes back to the problem of discrimination and learning to distinguish between the laws of man and the laws of God. Whilst it is not right to take another's karma from him we can, nonetheless, help him to bear the burden of it.

The quality of soul-consciousness developing through human experience is not gathered in one incarnation and likewise a series of incarnations is not spent on one lesson alone. Usually we have many lessons to learn in a particular incarnation. It is not that we pass one initiation, after so many incarnations, and then another after some more lives. It is more likely that there is a general development, from the various lessons being learnt in many incarnations, which then culminate in a series of initiations in one life. On the other hand, it may be that an initiation is taken in a particular life and then a whole sequence of lives passes before the next initiation can take place.

Spiritual evolution is a perfect procedure - the pieces of various lives are used and brought together like the parts of a jigsaw to form a perfect pattern of man's life on earth.

19

HELP FROM HIGHER REALMS

Our life is what our thoughts make it.
Marcus Aurelius

There is a plan for all our lives. We are like children who have come back to school and our own soul, although its memory has faded for the time being, sub-consciously knows we have come here to gain certain knowledge. Daily life which seems so irksome at times and our bodies which are occasionally so tiresome to maintain are, in reality, the restrictions from which we learn. Overcoming the frustration of daily living is the experience we need to help us build the soul qualities which must be developed before we can be free from the bondage of physical life.

Subconsciously most of us long for a better world. There is, in some way, an attachment to the life of spirit and rightly so because it is our true home. Our intuition tells us that we come from a more beautiful place for a purpose and according to a plan. We have come from the world of spirit to live in the flesh where we are imprisoned until we learn to free ourselves. This does not mean freedom through death because death does not necessarily set us free from bondage. The freedom is best achieved whilst we are here on earth. The release from the limitations of our baser natures and physical cravings has to be achieved by our own efforts. However, having let go of these restrictions we can, whilst still in our earthly incarnation, enter into the heaven realms of peace, serenity, beauty and joy. This can be achieved in meditation and at other moments of attunement with nature.

On this seemingly interminable journey and long pilgrimage of incarnations you may well ask who can best help us? We are assured that guidance is available, from the higher realms, from both angelic and human sources. The guardian angel is the messenger sent by the Creator from the heavenly states to help each of us through all our various experiences of life on earth. Your guardian angel never leaves you and is the helper of the soul when, and if, it desires to be helped. Strength and guidance are available on request as it were.

The guardian angel is, of course, present at the time of birth and always cares for that reincarnating soul. We must remember that the angelic beings have never experienced human incarnation and, until man is able to control his emotions, they are unable to draw very close. The guardian angel may attempt to draw close but it is only in its tranquil moments that the soul is receptive to the ministry of angels. Often we are so concerned with the events around us that we are deaf to the prompting of our guardian angel. The human guidance comes from a particular teacher or guide, human in origin but now in spirit, who may be attached to us through a number of lives. That guide is aware of the problems of earthly life and understands the sorrows and human weaknesses common to every living soul. The guide also knows that in the course of evolution all will emerge strong and radiant, victorious over the difficulties and conflicts of earthly life.

These discarnate guides, from their higher perspective, see us as radiant souls struggling to learn what we must. Our teacher or guide will have a number of helpers who, in turn, come to help us through particularly difficult periods and trials or tribulations of one sort or another. Access to such helpers, with a special knowledge of certain subjects, is possible. An artist might be inspired by a skilled artist now in spirit, a writer, musician or doctor likewise. When a particular skill is being used in this life expertise, from discarnate souls with experience in such matters, is on tap from the spirit world. Many people get inspiration from such sources quite unconsciously. Sometimes these helpers are also called guides and this is a little confusing. However, we can listen to our true guide, who comes from a different level than the helpers, through the voice of our higher self or what we might call our conscience. It is helpful to be attuned to this voice from above.

As already suggested the karma most of us have created in past lives, through our actions and thoughts, has the effect that very few of us enjoy the degree of free-will one might imagine. Our choice is limited - probably by fixations of thought which are the legacy of our early environment. In the big events of life such as birth, marriage, work, environment, travel, health, it may seem that we have a conscious decision to make but the reality is different. The choice is very often made, long before, at a deeper level. Our guardian angel who, as discussed earlier; is always with us at these outwardly crucial moments of decision, ensures that we follow the path previously chosen by our higher self before incarnating. Hence the importance of turning inwards, at all times. in order to attune to the help available.

Our real free-will lies in the inner realms of thought and feeling. We have free-will to choose how we think and how we react to people and circumstances. Deep within every soul, in the heart centre, there shines a light which is our link with the Creator. We can choose whether to try to become more aware of that light, that divine self, which urges us to treat others as we would like to be treated. Alternatively, we can allow ourselves to be held down by material and selfish considerations until such time that the inner light is practically smothered, covered by layers of selfish desire and thoughtlessness.

Every time the soul consciously chooses to rise in spirit towards the light, the good, the true or the beautiful, the law of opportunity works to create a more harmonious environment for the future. This may take the form of a healthier body and a greater capacity to serve. No matter how difficult our present circumstances may be, every soul has the opportunity to sow, now, a golden harvest for the future.

Most of us are familiar with the expression that *everything comes right in the end.* We are assured that it must and does come right - so why should we be fearful? There are times in our lives when we appear to have more than our fair share of difficulties but still manage to remain calm and positive. At other times we can be overwhelmed and become very negative. By surrendering to the will of the Creator - *going with the flow,* we will find things a great deal easier. Assurance is given that we will always receive gentle and loving help from those in the world of light. They are always ready to do something which brings us blessing and compensation - that's if we give them half a chance! So, despite the hard knocks through which we receive our lessons, we will also receive compensation and blessing from the unseen.

We are not forgotten. The help is available but we need to remember that those on the other side can only descend so far. It is all a matter of vibration, harmony and attunement. Earth is of a slow vibration. Mortal man has to quicken his vibration to become attuned. He must raise himself to meet and greet his spirit friends. On the one hand, it is all so simple and so clear and yet, on the other hand, so profound and so difficult to attain. In spirit, as on earth, only *keeping on keeping on* will ensure our progress.

20

THE PENDULUM SWINGS

For love is the beauty of the soul.
In so much as love grows in you, so in you beauty grows.
Saint Augustine

Written over the entrance to many an ancient mystery school were the words: *Man, know thyself and thou shalt know God and the Universe.* This was a succinct way of expressing the ancient principle *as above, so below, as in heaven, so on earth.* We can only begin to understand this wonderful principle when we realise that the whole manifested universe is the result of the thought of the Creator. As we are made in this image we all possess deep within our souls a measure of this same creative power. The light, which shines in all our hearts, links us with the great sun of our universe and with the spiritual power at the heart of this galaxy. The truth is that man is a creator in the making, a universe in miniature.

Astrologers well know the extraordinary and mysterious linking of people's character and circumstances with the position in the heavens of the sun, moon and planets at the moment of birth. The sacred science of astrology is inherent in all religions. The signs may have different symbols, different names in different cultures but basically they all demonstrate the truth of the soul's evolution from the animal to the human and ultimately to the divine self.

This principal *as above, so below as in heaven, so on earth* is also a law of externalisation and thus our inner thoughts and feelings build from the past to the body we have now. That body is our instrument for service at the moment. Those same thoughts and feelings also influence our destiny. The inner thoughts and feelings imprint themselves upon the physical body, as in the lines of the palm, the contours of the head and in every form of the body's expression such as handwriting, posture and gait. In the innermost self there is a programme showing how our life will unfold and this programme is evident in every part of the body. Particularly observant doctors can usually diagnose, according to physical type and build, the disease to which patients are likely to succumb. A trained seer who understands how to interpret the signs, would be able to judge quite accurately a soul's character and destiny during the present life.

Again in the words *as above, so below, as in heaven, so on earth* we have a key to the study of spiritual science. As we begin to learn more of the full implications of this law and the exactitude with which it works, we cannot but wonder at the majesty of divine wisdom behind every detail of human life. There is a law of balance and equilibrium apparent everywhere in nature. It is the law of opposites - yin and yang. The balance between day and night, heat and cold, expansion and contraction, positive and negative currents, acid and alkali and so on. As a pendulum swings one way it must then swing the other. This law governs every aspect of our lives - the soul plane as well as in the physical body.

To gain necessary experience the soul needs to incarnate, sometimes in a male and sometimes in a female body. However, this change of sex does not necessary occur in each alternate life. We may have a series of incarnations, either in a male or female body, in order to gain a thorough experience of the needs and qualities of both or because of some special mission of the soul. Then the pendulum swings back and we start a series of lives in the opposite type of body.

This swinging of the pendulum of life between the two can, perhaps, give us a greater sympathy and understanding for souls who are at the point of change - which can manifest as homosexuality. The change into a different type of body, after a run of incarnations in the same sex, may make it difficult, at first, for the individual to be released from the pull of that sex which has been theirs for a number of lives. The fact that many great artists are, or have been, homosexual may indicate a time when the soul, to some extent, lives more in the inner world and can be particularly responsive to angelic inspiration in the arts or sciences. In the spirit world a woman has opportunity for maternal expression, for which her soul might long, particularly if she had been denied that opportunity in a previous live. Equally, a man can pursue the creative arts for which he may have longed, consciously or subconsciously, over many years.

This fundamental law of balance, which affects both mind and body, acts as a safeguard to the soul ensuring that any kind of extremism can only be carried so far - before reaction sets in and pulls us back to normal. This law can cause the personality to swing, in successive incarnations, between introvert and extrovert until such time as a perfectly balanced expression is reached.

Any kind of fanaticism in one incarnation could lead to similar fanaticism, in the opposite direction, in another incarnation. This can be particularly true in questions of religious or racial bigotry. For instance, a puritanical soul, demanding complete simplicity in one life may come back with equal religious fanaticism in the next but, this time, demanding elaborate ceremonial practices. A persecutor of coloured races could well be born in the very race which had been the object of his persecution.

Always we receive as we have given, the swing of the pendulum ensuring that we are drawn into an opposite experience in order to widen our understanding and bring the soul into complete balance. So we learn to reach the heights and plumb the depths of human experience. Gradually we grow in wisdom, tolerance, compassion and humour until we can truly understand the meaning and the joy of the brotherhood of all life.

21

DESTINY, FREE-WILL AND DYING.

Love nothing but that which comes to you woven in the pattern of
your destiny. For what could more aptly fit your needs?
Marcus Aurelius

Many people do not believe that our lives are predestined. In
fact they are, or pretty much so. There is a plan for our lives.
Our destiny is a result of our own plan for this life, decided
before incarnation and of our free-will. Nonetheless this life
plan can be influenced by someone else's plan for our life and,
of course, the free-will of others.

As stated in an earlier chapter before coming into incarnation
again there is that period of peace and quiescence, of rest and
recuperation. When we shed our physical body at the end of a
particular incarnation the soul sees a picture of its whole
journey so far. The decision is then made as to what further
experience and growth is needed. That is where the real free-
will is manifest. The soul may, perhaps, choose an easy life or
it may be given such a vision of the ultimate perfection that it
longs to clear its debts quickly, so that it may become one with
that heavenly beauty and peace. In this case it may choose a very
difficult incarnation, perhaps with a severely handicapped body

or mind, or one in which there is almost unbearable emotional strain and suffering.

We seem to be able to manoeuvre, to some extent, within the broad plan by our reactions to the events around us. By the same token someone else may change the plan for us by utilising their free-will to react in a particular way. If someone else changes the plan for us they will incur karmic liability on our behalf. Whether, or not, we are conscious of these things is another matter. However, when we plan our lives, events such as floods, hurricanes, earthquakes, etc. are known to be possibilities by our higher mind, or intuition, long before they happen and they are taken into account.

When death comes the soul detaches itself from the body and the silver cord is severed completely. That is the beginning and end of the mechanics of death. There are, of course, a few minor conditions involved. It seems no soul can ever pass over into those subtle worlds unless it has given it's consent. This does not mean conscious consent because the conscious mind is only a minor extension of the soul. The conscious mind may assume that death is approaching but it is the soul itself that must acquiesce before the process can take place.

One wonders if it is right to try to prolong the lives of the old who are tired and only want to die? But, as already suggested, passing over from this world to the next can only be done with the consent of the soul of the individual concerned. A doctor may think he is prolonging the life of his patient but this is outside his control. In effect he is waiting for his patient to give the necessary consent to his own release. It is clear that nobody can keep a person alive longer that the Creator has ordained. Even if the body has no further need of life, the soul might not yet be ready to set in motion the complex procedures of incarnation. Thus life lingers on.

During sleep our souls can travel to ethereal planes whilst maintaining contact with our mortal bodies by a thin silver thread. The bible calls this the *silver cord*. It anchors the soul to the body until the need for sleep has been satisfied. Sometimes a recollection of the soul's journey, in the form of a very vivid dream, filters down this *silver cord* and in to the mind of the sleeper. But the human mind is fallible, having been conditioned since childhood to certain beliefs, and so the message transmitted by the silver cord can become garbled and incoherent. As a result we might experience some ghastly nightmare and wake up in a cold sweat of terror. On the assumption that the cause is not indigestion then possibly it is our soul observing us giving consideration to something contrary to divine will!

So far as death is concerned the bible talks about *the silver cord being severed and* the *golden bowl broken* which is both descriptive and symbolic - signifying the end of the earth experience, at least for the time being. Nature wraps us in a blanket. An individual, even if he is terrified of dying, merely falls asleep. In his sleep, he dreams that he is still in the same room though he is, in fact, passing to the *golden world*. The actual act of dying is as simple as dozing off to sleep after lunch. One esoteric source describes it thus:

A drowsy feeling fills your whole body with relaxing comfort. You can still see, with your earthly eyes, the room about you. Then you notice that there are all kinds of new people standing about your bed, people that you once knew; such as parents, a favourite uncle, a friend who passed over many years sooner;

the joy of seeing them again takes your mind off everything else. They take you by the hand and lift you to your feet. This invariably causes you to look back at the bed and to your surprise you, or rather your mortal shell, is still lying there. You say aloud 'But how can I be here with you people, and yet still be lying here on the bed?' Only then do you realise that this is death.

So now you are taken by your friends to the world where you now belong. As you move out of the room together, you pass through what appears to be a fog or a mist. It is not dense and you can see a little way ahead of you. Since you know and love the people you are with, you follow them gladly. The mist is caused by the dispersing of your etheric body, which has served as the guardian of your material body. The etheric body, now that death has intervened, leaves the material body and seeks to attach itself to the soul. But as you move up towards the rarer planes, the etheric body is unable to follow and it forms the mist which obscures your vision for a few seconds. When you step out of the mist, the etheric matter returns to the universal reservoirs.

In the case of a person who is familiar with the process of death the situation is a little different. The conscious passing over of someone would be restricted to very few people in the Western world today. Mostly these would be advanced souls who returned to earth only to perform a specific task, to bring about an advance in thought or encourage a particular philosophy. When the time comes for them to return to the higher realm, they do so with the utmost relief and joy. They tidy up their earthly affairs, then unhurriedly ask the blessings of the Creator. Then they simply lift out of their bodies and come straight to the plane where they belong. Nothing could be simpler and more benign.

A further means of passing over is by accident. Although the conscious mind does not know it is about to return, the soul does. In some cases it may be some days or weeks when, subconsciously, one knows that a particular earth life is coming to an end. Actual passing involves no pain or shock as already discussed and, as covered in subsequent chapters, even if it appears violent from here it is not so from other end.

In the case of a rather backward soul he or she is likely to be put into a dormant state on arrival in the heavenly world. The individual would wake up to what appears to be a hospital ward. Slowly the realisation that all is well would permeate that being. Gradually it dawns on the person that there are no doctors or nurses in this hospital or, for that matter, no bandages or surgical instruments. No pain is felt so the next move is likely to be exploring the surroundings. The need is to find out what sort of hospital it is. Only then the realisation that he or she has successfully passed over dawns. The helpers look on with pleasure at the amazement and relief demonstrated when the individual finds him or herself more alive than ever. It takes some time, quite some time, for all of this to register completely.

Quite often the first reaction of the newcomer is to go back to bed for a few days to get used to the idea of what has happened. After that one of the elders is likely to visit and answer all the unasked questions. Obviously the laws of creation are not as easily grasped by backward souls as they would be by their more experienced brothers.

Now imagine the case of an elderly person with a reasonable faith in the Creator. Let us say this person had been a fairly good Christian during life, trying to live the laws as they were laid down by the Master Jesus. Admittedly the odd law was broken when temptation became too great but the feeling, in his or her own mind, is that the Creator will forgive the everyday minor transgressions. In fact that would not be a correct assumption because in that sense *there is no judgement* when one passes over into the next, or real world. The soul vibrates at a certain rate and when it passes over it will vibrate at a similar rate. If, for example, one has led a deceitful life on earth then the soul vibrations will be somewhat sluggish and one will go to a *low* plane on the *other side*. One's companions there will be similar in mind and deed. Imagine the in-fighting that goes on among such people but there will be nobody to play judge. Instead one meets the application of the law: *As you sow, so shall you reap.* We judge ourselves.

Suicide is not recommended. There are, of course, infinite variations but, in general terms according to some esoteric sources, when the soul of a suicide victim arrives on the other side it is immediately placed in a state of rest until the associated horrors of the suicide have gone away. The unfortunate individual may soon find himself or herself back on earth to inhabit a new body with no recollection of the previous existence. In the new life, however, the same problems will confront that person until he or she learns to face those particular difficulties rather than trying to escape them. For all that the individual will be surrounded by the love of the Creator and guarded by his or her brothers. But problems need to be solved without aid from anyone and once these have been faced and resolved there is no further danger of committing suicide. It is important to realise that when you look at any human being you are looking at a child of God.

If there was not enough love in the heart of a new arrival in the heaven world then the ability of that soul to adapt to a world that operates on love would be compromised. This is just as well because the first thing an unloving soul might do would be to create weapons and then use them to establish power over fellow beings. Fortunately, however, such individuals could not hurt one another as their new bodies are indestructible. It does not take long for such people to realise the futility of picking up a weapon and thumping a neighbour over the head. Whilst they might feel very hard done by they end up realising that they will only progress by living in peace with their fellows. Gradually, unselfish gestures emerge and, finally, the texture of the soul purifies itself enough to reach a more peaceful plane. As things become clearer to them they advance to higher and yet more harmonious planes of existence.

We are told that it is much more dangerous and unpleasant to be born into the earthly world than it is to leave it. Being born is a painful, risky process. Nobody contemplates it with any degree of pleasure. And yet many people on earth fear death! Death is a great adventure and we should welcome our release from earthly bondage. We step out of the prison gates and into the sunlight.

22

DEATH AND NEAR DEATH EXPERIENCES

As soon as one belongs to a narrow creed in science every
unprejudiced and true perception is gone.
Goethe

There is no scientific proof of life after death. Equally there is
no scientific way of proving a person has toothache or many
other things for that matter. Science puts up a premise and then
goes about proving or disproving it. If I claimed I had
toothache this would not amount to scientific proof. Scientifically I would not have toothache. There is no way of measuring
it. My protestations of being in pain is a private experience and
subjective.

In the 15th century Copernicus, the Polish astronomer, demonstrated that the planets, including the earth, revolve around the
sun. Prior to that people had believed that the earth was
stationary and the other planets revolved around it. Nothing had
changed it was simply a question of seeing things differently.
However, it was really about 200 years ago when Science upset
the apple cart and created doubts about what we should or
should not believe. Evidence began to be interpreted differently. Science was at odds with religion. Both are rigid systems.

139

Science would have the greatest difficulty in measuring love, beauty, good, evil, feeling, or morality (or toothache!). Religion was not meant to be questioned - just followed! Science, perhaps, has a problem in accepting that the mind (not the brain) is separate from and superior to the body. Again we move into a difficult area if scientific proof is needed.

I have already stated that there is no scientific proof of life after death but what about *near death experiences?* These are experiences that many people have had after a severe accident or when they have been seriously ill. When these *near death experiences* occur the individual is *out of his body, in a state of peace and completely without pain.* After such experiences individuals speak of a shining world inhabited by beings of light. They speak of meeting deceased relatives or friends. Occasionally they are aware of having reviewed their lives. A barrier or fog can block progress beyond *a point of no return* and a decision is taken to return to the physical body.

Again there is little scientific approval but, despite the lack of proof of these near death experiences, there is much evidence if one accepts the universality of such events. Millions of people have had such experiences irrespective of colour, race or religion. The *near death experience* is very real and, indeed, greater reality is felt than in the normal world. The experiences are inexplicable in medical terms.

There is a small but growing acceptance of empirical experience of a similar kind. For example individuals are able to describe in great detail, from a vantage point outside of their physical body, everything that happens to them while undergoing an operation or during resuscitation, etc. Interestingly enough, on the scientific front, recent trials on near death experiences carried out by a Dr Schumaccher in the USA, demonstrate that individuals have a flat encephalographic reading (electrical reading of brain activity) whilst out of their bodies.

I have a video tape called VISIONS OF HOPE which is about *near death experiences.* The video amounts to a series of interviews, with about a dozen individuals, all of whom have had these experiences. In the various interviews there is a remarkable consensus about what happens when one is considered to be *dead.* The feeling of peace, light, serenity and love prevails throughout.

One man spoke of his experiences as a child in hospital. His parents were told by the doctor - 'he's gone'. The post mortem arrangements had been put in progress but at that time he was *outside his body, above it and looking down from the ceiling.* He was *attached to his body by a blue, silvery cord.* He then experienced *absolute peace and serenity and was aware of the brightest light ever experienced.* He was *also aware of the appearance of a being and he looked down and saw a ball turning in space.* He did not want to go back to what he later realised was the earth planet but he was *made aware that he ought to do so.* As he journeyed back in space he saw the colours of the earth and *impacted* with it (this was long before the space shots revealed the sort of picture one might expect to see from space). He went on to make a full recovery and the experience made him realise that there is *no such thing as death.*

Another person spoke of being very ill in hospital when she was in her 20's watching her body from above the bed and then experiencing a *luminous white light with blue in the middle - absolute peace and beauty* and she spoke of a *light at the end of a tunnel* which she wanted to follow. She was then aware of a presence or voice which posed the question - *have you really done everything you want to do?* She was also aware of a demarcation line at which point one could go on into the light or *be sucked back again to earthly existence.* She felt it was not time to give up her earthly responsibilities and woke up to find herself covered with tubes, drips and other paraphernalia associated with hospital intensive care procedures. For her it took away the fear associated with death and enabled her to get on with life in a much more meaningful way.

A woman talked about experiencing a bad attack of influenza. She was unable to swallow and was hospitalised. Later she was unable to speak and barely conscious. Lying in her hospital bed she was aware of *going up in another dimension* and *seeing a beautiful landscape, moving columns of light, lovely colours, music, but not in the way we understand it.* The atmosphere of *love and activity* made it very desirable but, again, there was an awareness that this was not her time to be there and she spoke of coming back, reluctantly, into her body *through a dark, damp canal.*

Another man had a *near death experience* after a severe illness. He had a *sensation of falling* and came to in a *place of light and brightness* where he said he *had never felt so alive.* He recognised some old friends there whom he knew to be dead. He was *very happy and did not want to leave.* He was *persuaded* to return and had the unfortunate sensation of *coming to* on a mortuary shelf where he sat up and said *where am I?* Since the mortuary attendant was rather shocked by this experience *the corpse* felt obliged to get off his shelf and obtain a glass of water for the attendant! After a lot of nursing, following the experience of being *dead* for half an hour, during which time the funeral arrangements had been put in progress, this individual made a full recovery. He went on to say how reluctant he had been to leave *that wonderful place* and for him the *best is yet to be.* All fear of death has gone.

Of her near death experience another woman said the *nearer I got to the light the feeling of love increased.* She would have liked to have stayed there...the peace and love she felt was beyond explanation.

A woman who was in severe pain at the age of 28 was hospitalised and had her head packed in ice in order to relieve the pain. She felt herself...*rising out of the pain like a balloon going up and was aware of floating up to just below the ceiling.* It was *very calm and there was an incredible feeling of light.* Looking down from her vantage point near the ceiling she *saw her body intact on the bed below and also she saw her husband enter the room and lay his body across her tummy, sobbing silently.* She became aware of her responsibilities to her children and felt, reluctantly, that she must go back to look after the family. Her new awareness has given her an entirely different view of life.

Dr. Kubler Ross, who has written a great deal on the subject of *near death experiences* speaks of 20,000 such cases and has experienced one herself. She was aware of *light at the end of a tunnel and of such peace and love... and goes on to say that when you come back from such an experience everything is changed.*

23

COMMUNICATIONS FROM THE SUMMERLAND

Deliver us from these human forms and reclothe us in light
amongst the stars.
Nosairi Prayer

Having acquainted the reader with the notion of a non-physical world and the fact that individuals from those realms can communicate with us I would like to give some examples of the experiences of various people. In order to do so I have taken extracts from three different books about life in the *Summerland.* As already indicated this is the name given to the realm we go to soon after death. I think it better to use the original words used by the individuals concerned and thus I am quoting the appropriate extracts as they were originally published.

There are many books dealing with such channelled information. I have selected some which are not particularly recent to make the point that this not a new phenomenon. The first quote is from a book called PRIVATE DOWDING containing information communicated to the author Wellesley Tudor Pole. It was first published in 1917 by The Pilgrim Press. I can do no better than repeat the introduction to the book by W.T.P. and that reads as follows:

On Monday, 12th March 1917, I was walking by the sea when I felt the presence of someone. I looked round; no one was in sight. All that day I felt as if someone was following me, trying to reach my thoughts. Suddenly I said to myself: 'It is a soldier. He has been killed in battle and wants to communicate!' That evening I happened to call upon a lady who possesses some degree of clairvoyant power. I had forgotten about the soldier, until she described a man dressed in khaki, sitting in a chair near me. He was gazing intently in my direction. She said he was mature, wore a small moustache, and seemed somewhat sad. Not a very intelligent character apparently, but an honest one.

I came home and sat down at my writing table. Immediately my pen moved. Did I move it? Yes, in an involuntary sort of way. The thoughts were not my own, the language was a little unusual. Ideas were mainly conveyed in short simple phrases. It would really seem as if some intelligence outside myself was speaking through my mind and my pen. Some of the ideas were not in conformity with preconceived notions of my own. The messages I received in this manner from Thomas Dowding, recluse, schoolmaster and soldier, are set down exactly as they reached me.

In the book about Private Dowding this first communication with W.T.P. is dated March 12, 1917 at 9pm. I will not quote it all because it is lengthy but I will detail the first eight paragraphs. These are as follows:

I am grateful for this opportunity. You may not realise how much some of us long to speak to those we have left behind. It is not easy to get messages through with certainty. They are so often lost in transit or misinterpreted. Sometimes the imagina-

tion of the receiver weaves a curious fabric round the thoughts we try to pass down, then the ideas we want to communicate are either lost or disfigured.

I was a schoolmaster in a small east coast town before the war. I was an orphan, somewhat of a recluse and I made friends but slowly. My name is of no importance; apparently names over here are not needed. I became a soldier in the autumn of 1915 and left my narrow village life behind. These details, however, are really of no importance. They may act as a background to what I have to say. I joined as a private and died as a private. My soldiering lasted just nine months, eight of which were spent training in Northumberland.

I went out with my battalion to France in July 1916 and we went into the trenches almost at once. I was killed by a shell splinter one evening in August and I believe my body was buried the following day. As you see, I hasten over these unimportant events, important to me once, but now of no real consequence. How we overestimate the significance of earthly ties.

Well my body soon became cannon fodder and there were few to mourn me. It was not for me to play anything but an insignificant part in this world-tragedy, which is still unfolding.

I am still myself, a person of no importance but I feel I should like to say a few things before passing along. I feared death but that was natural. I was timid and even feared life and its pitfalls. So I was afraid of being killed and was more sure it would mean extinction. There are still many who believe that. It is because extinction has not come to me that I want to speak to you. May I describe my experiences? Perhaps they may *prove useful to some. How necessary that some of us should speak back across the border! The barriers must be broken down. This is one of the ways of doing it. Listen therefore to what I have to say:*

Physical death is nothing. There really is no cause for fear. Some of my pals grieved for me. When I went West they thought I was dead for good. This is what happened. I have a perfectly clear memory of the whole incident. I was waiting at the corner of a traverse to go on guard. It was a fine evening. I had no special intimation of danger until I heard the whiz of a shell. Then followed an explosion, somewhere behind me. I crouched down involuntarily but was too late. Something struck hard, hard, hard, against my neck. Shall I ever lose the memory of that hardness? It is the only unpleasant incident that I can remember. I fell and as I did so, without passing through any apparent interval of unconsciousness, I found myself outside myself! You see I am telling my story simply; you will find it easier to understand. You will learn to know what a small incident dying is.

Think of it! One moment I was alive, in the earthly sense, looking over a trench parapet un-alarmed, normal. Five seconds later I was standing outside my body, helping two of my pals to carry my body down the trench labyrinth towards a dressing station. They thought I was senseless but alive. I did not know whether I had jumped out of my body through shell shock, temporarily or forever. You see what a small thing is death, even the violent death of war! I seemed in a dream. I had dreamt that someone or something had knocked me down. Now I was dreaming that I was outside my body. Soon I should wake up and find myself in the traverse waiting to go on guard It all happened so simply. Death was for me a simple experience - no horror, no long-drawn suffering, no conflict. It came to many in the same way. My pals need not fear death. Few of them do, nevertheless there is an underlying dread of possible extinction. I dreaded that; many soldiers do, but they rarely have time to think about such things. As in my case, thousands of soldiers pass over without knowing it. If there be shock, it is not the shock of physical death. Shock comes later when comprehension dawns: Where is my body? Surely I am not dead! In my own case I knew nothing more than I have already related, at the time. When I found that my two pals could carry my body without my help, I dropped behind; I just followed, in a curiously humble way. Humble? Yes, because I seemed so useless. We met a stretcher party. My body was hoisted on to the stretcher. I wondered when I should get back into it again. You see, I was so little dead that I imagined I was still (physically) alive. Think of it a moment before we pass on. I had been struck by a shell splinter. There was no pain. The life was knocked out of my body; again, I say there was no pain. Then I found that the whole of myself. All, that is, that thinks and sees and feels and knows was still alive and conscious! I had begun a new chapter of life. I will tell you what I felt like. It was as if I had been running hard until, hot and breathless, I had thrown my overcoat away. The coat was my body and if I had not thrown it away I should have been suffocated. I cannot describe the experience in any better way; there is nothing else to describe.

My body went to the first dressing station and after examination was taken to the mortuary. I stayed near it all that night, watching but without thoughts. It was as if my being, feeling, and thinking had become suspended by some Power outside myself. This sensation came over me gradually as the night advanced. I still expected to wake up in my body again, that is so far as I expected anything. Then I lost consciousness and slept soundly.

As the story of Private Dowding continues one learns that he gradually becomes more aware of his situation and he eventually is able to communicate all sorts of helpful information. Despite his unassuming and modest manner the work he is given to do is of the utmost importance.

In another book called THE AWAKENING LETTERS compiled by Rosamond Lehmann and Cynthia Sandys the text of many communications from various individuals, who have passed on, are detailed. The book was first published in 1978 by Neville Spearman (Jersey) Ltd., now at Saffron Walden, Essex. The bulk of the material is from Cynthia's brother Joe who, prior to death, was Sir Alvary Gascoigne.

Cynthia Sandy's preparation for mental mediumship was utterly simple and unassuming. The following is a quote from the Forward to the book written by Rosamond Lehmann and describing the procedure Cynthia followed to make herself ready to receive the *letters:*

Having disposed of her many household chores, she sits quietly, her writing pad on her lap and after a period of deep meditation, takes up a pen and starts to write. She gives the impression of intense yet effortless concentration while she takes down what her spiritual hearing is receiving. The words come in an uninterrupted, unpunctuated flow.

To give the reader a flavour of that book the first quote is part of a *letter* from Sir Alvary Gascoigne. It is entitled THE TYCOON and begins as follows:

I *asked Pat what happens to the millions of people who come*
over with no one in their entourage to help? Her reply was:
'Come and see'. So I found myself in a rather rich house, with
an old man just passing out of his earth body. He had been a
real tycoon in industry and was very rich. His poor old wife
couldn't face life without him. He'd always done everything
and now she was alone. I sensed that they had no children and
he'd been so successful that he'd alienated most of his contem-
poraries and there he stood outside his body, a grey frightened
individual completely alone. I went up to him and spoke some
sort of welcome to show he wasn't quite alone. He heard me,
looked round the room and merely grunted,
'How the devil did you get in?'
I laughed and tried to explain, pointing to his corpse on the bed.
'What have you done to me?' was his next remark. 'Have you
killed me?'
'No' I repeated, 'you must remember your illness'
He nodded.
'Well now you have died according to the doctor but you can
see there is no death only a change of body; how do you feel?'
'I don't know who you are and you have no right to be here - get
out'.
'Of course, if you say so,' I replied, 'but then you will be
quite alone'
'No, I didn't mean that, you can stay, you are only a voice
anyhow.' Then he began to see me. 'Oh you're not only a voice
you are a man! Well how do you see me and my wife doesn't?
Can you tell me that?'
'Yes'..I replied, 'you are an etheric now; you have left your
physical body forever.'
'That can't be true, this is just a dream and a very worrying one
too and I'll wake up in a moment.' Then he went over to the bed
and tried to overlay his body, but it was cold and repellent.

'Can't do it' he said in desperation. *'Well come and help me whoever you are. Anyway, I'm not dead'.*

But he was so exhausted that I was able to persuade him to lie on a sofa in his own room and in a moment he was asleep. The account continues with an amusing description of the tycoon's difficulty in appreciating his death and his eventual understanding of the situation as he meets an old friend who had passed on in the previous year.

The following is another letter taken from the same book - this time it is from a country doctor who was a general practitioner:

May I write? I was a doctor on earth and I knew you intimately, my name is Sykes. I was very fond of you all, but I had no use for religion or faith healing, or any of those sentimental emotions. Pain was far too real to be tackled like that. I suffered and came over in a rather battered state of mind. There seemed to be so much useless suffering and unhappiness and it seemed to be all without rhyme or reason. Then I woke up in a hospital. I had died at home and could not think how I'd got there. But it was a most wonderful place. I became instantly so much excited by what I saw and felt that I had no idea that I was looking at etheric treatment.A doctor came over to me, and asked how I was feeling adding; 'We shall be glad to teach you all we know.' Well, I wasn't asking anything except in my own mind, but he was answering my unspoken thought. I found myself wondering if my blood pressure could be taken and he replied at once, 'Yes, if you like, but we don't need to here, the blood circulates quite differently'. What did he mean?

He sat down beside me and out of nowhere a diagram appeared showing the organs and arteries of my new body. 'This is what you've got to work on now,' he explained. I thought I must be going mad. Here was a diagram of a body, similar in shape to the one I knew, but with feeding ducts, digestive organs and so on, of a much simpler kind. I noticed all the pressure points of the body were marked with 'light intake', 'colour intake', 'heat intake' and so on. The digestive organs seemed to be on a rotary system. It looked like one large fly-wheel that drew in from all sides the white and coloured rays, transforming them into energy and life such as I am now experiencing. After a few moments he sensed that I couldn't take in any more. The diagram vanished and I slept - thinking, thinking, thinking!

The next thing that I remember was hearing music, lovely deep music like a church organ. I felt as though it was putting strength and weight into me. If I had felt light-headed before that had now gone. I was being fed, that was the sensation, definitely fed on music and when I became replete I slept again. May I write again some time?

Finally, in this chapter, I would like to take a quotation from a book called THE GOLDEN KEY by Percy Wexford, first published in 1927 by White Eagle Publishing Trust. This book contains letters from Percy to his grandmother Mrs Ethel Wexford. Percy had died in his mid-twenties after a short illness. (His brother George, serving in The Royal Flying Corps, had been killed 10 years earlier while flying over enemy lines in 1916.)

Within 8 days of his death Percy began communicating the first of a series of letters through Grace Cooke (see chapter 12). She was a well known and highly regarded person who was later chosen as the medium through whom Sir Arthur Conan Doyle, creator of the fictional detective hero Sherlock Holmes, was able to communicate about life after death. That remarkable story is described in detail in a book called THE RETURN OF ARTHUR CONAN DOYLE.

Percy's letters start with a description of waking up and being *astounded* to see George, his brother, standing at his side. He found it was very hard to believe that he was really dead. The letters are fascinating - full of information about life in Summerland. To give you a flavour of this I will quote just part of a letter which was communicated about four months after his demise:

You have given me quite a nice lot of questions which I shall be pleased to answer if I can find the words to describe these spiritual things to you. In your first question you ask what is the purpose of our life over here? You said the purpose or culmination of life on earth was death. In the first place this is entirely wrong. The culmination of your life on earth is an awakening from a dream to a reality.

I have not been here long enough to know a great deal about the ultimate end of our life here but I have been told by my guide that all is working for a Perfecting of Life. I cannot tell you the realms of perfection we may attain. I know that this life is an eternal progression and we are working and living, striving after goodness, beauty and love. We are learning to become in the course of time perfect children of God when, I am told, we shall be 'One with the Father.' This cannot happen in a few short years but before us lie great periods of time as you understand it. But you must, in grasping these truths, realise that where the Spirit is concerned there is no limitation of time - that belongs to a world of matter.

The life of an individual spirit is rather like the development of the bloom from the seed placed in the earth passing through the various stages of growth until it issues forth in all its beauty with it's message to all who love it. So it is with the life of the Spirit. It is a gradual unfolding from darkness to sunshine. Then when it is perfected, it begins it's work of creating seeds as that from which it evolved. This is too great a subject for me to deal with. For my part I am perfectly contented with what I have seen of the beauty of this life here, to rest entirely happy in the knowledge of a God of infinite love and wisdom. Who, in the revelation which has been given to me since I was free from the earthly life, has proved to me that such a power as could conceive and create such perfection of life must have still greater and more perfect life to follow.

In the next two chapters I shall recount the events surrounding the deaths of two young people in different parts of the world. Their lives were cut short as a result of motoring *accidents.* The suggestion is that these events were not as haphazard or untimely as one might imagine. Judge for yourself.

24

An Accident?

What happens after death is so unspeakably glorious that our imagination and feelings do not suffice to form even an approximate conception of it.
Carl Jung

A young man called Mike Swain was driving along a road in South Africa together with a child companion, called Heather, when the car collided head on with another vehicle coming the other way. The two young people were killed instantly. Such tragedies happen every day on roads throughout the world. However, the story of this particular event, and its outcome, makes fascinating reading. It is contained in a book called ON THE DEATH OF MY SON by Jasper Swain, published by The Aquarian Press.

Mike's father, Jasper, was a South African lawyer, brought up an orthodox Christian in the Anglican faith. He had been quite a religious man but, at the time of the accident, he considered that organised religion no longer played a realistic part in modern society. Over the years he had investigated other religions including Lutheran, Catholic and Protestant as well as some of the lesser beliefs appealing only to minority groups. He had found all of them wanting in some respect. Jasper Swain had examined spiritualism and then turned to Hinduism, Mohammedism, Buddhism, Taoism and Zen and he was still unable to put his doubts to rest. At the time of the accident, although he was still searching, he had not arrived at any conclusions about his quest for knowledge in these matters.

After his son's funeral Jasper followed up a message which had been received by his secretary just after the accident. The message was from a Mrs Merrington who had telephoned from Sezela, quite some distance away from his home town of Pietermaritzburg. The message read as follows: *As you once helped her in life, she will now help you in death.* His initial response had been annoyance about this curious message and vexation at what he considered to be intrusion into his private grief. But, after the funeral, he could not get rid of a nagging thought in his mind about going to Sezela.

He finally gave in to the constant thought and drove to Sezela. There he found a large sugar-mill and having made some enquiries found out that Mr Merrington was one of the engineers there. On walking into Mr Merrington's office he was greeted with the words: *Ah you must be Jasper Swain. Mike told my wife to expect you here this morning. Not ten minutes ago she 'phoned me to be on the look out for you.* The bewildered Jasper soon met Mrs Merrington and remembered having met her nine years earlier when he had been a great help to her in some voluntary welfare connection.

As soon as she had installed Jasper into the sitting room she sat back and placed her two hands over her eyes. When she next spoke, Jasper heard his dead son addressing him as Chud, a

156

familiar name only used by his son Mike. The fascinating story that follows is contained in the book mentioned above. It is a remarkable account of the contact which began between Mike and his father and I shall quote some parts from it that I think are of special interest. I hope the words will be a comfort to anybody who has lost a close relation or friend in similar circumstances.

By putting the medium, Mrs Merrington, in the driver's seat, Mike was able, through her, to describe the fatal accident in great detail. The account reads as follows:

She began by saying: 'He has placed me in a small green Mini car. It has a peculiar gear lever, a short stubby gear lever, next to my left leg.' (The Mini had its normal gear shift altered, and a remote control gear shift had been mounted between the seats.) 'It is a terribly hot day and I am driving along a very crowded road. There is a little girl beside me. Her name is Heather. She is chatting to me about her mum and dad, who are in the car ahead of us. I can see their car, approximately fifty yards away. It is grey in colour, it looks like a Rambler. It is noon and there is a mass of holiday traffic passing us in both directions.'

/Now I see a black car coming towards us. As it approaches us, I see this other car coming behind it. I can see this other car clearly, because it is in the middle of the road, trying to pass the black car.' Mrs Merrington paused for a moment, and then said: 'The sun is glaring on the windscreen of the black car and reflecting back into my eyes. I can see nothing but a bright silver radiance. It is blinding me. All of a sudden, the radiance changes from silver to gold. I am being lifted up in the air, out through the top of the car. I grab little Heather's hand. She too is being lifted up out of the car.'

'We have been lifted thirty feet above the Mini. And in one horrifying second, I see the little Mini and this large car collide head-on. There is a noise like the snapping of steel banjo strings. The little Mini bounces right off the highway, right over onto the gravel verge. It is finally brought to a halt in a cloud of dust when it hits a giant ant-hill.'

'The large car is turning turtle in mid air. Its nose flips over until it is back to front. Then it smashes down onto the road on its side. Now it skids about four or five feet and finally it comes to a halt with an ear-splitting crash. A storm of metallic dust is now glinting all over the road. The wheels of this car are still spinning aimlessly.' Mrs Merrington stopped, obviously too agitated to continue. What impressed her listeners was the fact that Mike had never seen the other vehicle until after the silver light had changed to gold. He and Heather had felt no sense of impact. They had suffered no pain. Just a gentle ascent into the air.

Mrs Merrington recovered herself enough to continue: 'Heather and I are still holding hands. We now descend beside the Mini. We see two crumpled bodies lying in it. We feel vaguely sorry that this thing should have happened to them. And we both fully understand that we are, now, so far as mortals are concerned, dead. We are also both aware that a lot of people have begun to gather round us. They are dressed in glorious colours. We recognise familiar faces; the faces of friends who passed beyond the earth before us. We are still hand in hand; now, guided by the one who first lifted us into the air, the two of us sweep towards the skies. We drift above the two round hills known as the Breasts of Sheba.'

In heartfelt joy Jasper Swain listened, transported by the fact that the passing had involved neither fear, shock, nor suffering. During a later communication with Mike on the subject of whether or not the accident was planned or pre-ordained he had this to say: *'Oh yes, Dad! My death was okayed well ahead of the accident! To be exact, on the previous Monday, while I was watching the races at Kyalami, I suddenly knew that my life was coming to an end, even though I did not know the exact moment. I don't regret it, because I was also aware of the wonder, the love, and the beauty of the world that awaited me. Heather knew too. She was quite aware that the time was near. This is such a wonderful world, Dad. I wish I could describe the infinite beauty that surrounds us.'*

As the book ON THE DEATH OF MY SON unfolds the extraordinary and touching relationship between Jasper and his son is revealed which is a unique source of information about the life in the spiritual worlds.

25

ANOTHER ACCIDENT?

*Life between death and a new birth is as rich and varied as life
here between birth and death.*
Rudolf Steiner

Another young man, this time in England, was driving his motorcycle, in good visibility, along a familiar straight mile of dual carriageway when he failed to remember a minor road crossing. It was late on a Monday night when seventeen years old Peter Cowlin hit the rear of a car crossing slowly in his path. He sustained a moderate head injury and was later transferred to an intensive care unit. His injuries were serious but after some days he appeared to be making good progress and was moved to an orthopaedic ward. He was able to read the get well cards from friends, speak a few words and write a few more.

Visitors came and went but got little verbal response from him. Nursing staff were not unduly worried at this situation as his responses, when made, were logical and he was relaxed. Towards the end of the week, however, he seemed increasingly pre-occupied and he would smile as though in response to a conversation with a person or persons invisible to the various people around his bed.

On the Saturday following the accident the medical team were satisfied with his progress and he was taken off frequent monitoring. His mother was told *he will be all right* and that *he's fully conscious now.* Peter listened, his gaze incredulous, as if aware that he knew differently. Some hours later he began to vomit. The cardiac arrest team were called but within a few minutes Peter was *gone.*

The philosophy of Michael Cowlin, Peter's adopted father, was such that he was aware that it is only the physical body which suffers destruction at death and he was convinced that the essential Peter was near them still. Some months after the funeral, through a family friend who is a trance medium, Michael Cowlin was able to communicate with Peter. The subject of that communication is detailed in a remarkable book called TRUTH IS VEILED produced by Michael and June Cowlin and available from them. (see acknowledgements)

I shall quote from various parts of the book as we proceed but, once again, to comfort anybody who has lost a friend or relative in tragic circumstances, the following conversation between Peter Cowlin and his father, some 6 weeks or so after his demise may be of particular interest:

Peter: *Hello Dad, I'm not very far away from you. Let's have a conversation. On the day I had my accident I had been into Hemel to get my loudspeaker and parts. So I was very happy. I was thinking about this when I went through the lights. I just didn't remember them. The other car came across and I didn't see it till too late. I knew I was going to hit it and tried to ease back off the seat but it was too late. Everything seemed against me. Then I was out. When I woke up I could scarcely move. All my body hurt and my head seemed to have a great weight on it.*

Later, I felt better. But, then I started to feel bad again. Just before I lifted out of my body I felt terrible.

Michael Cowlin: *Directly after the accident you were unconscious. Can you remember anything of that period?*
Peter: *Yes, I went towards a great, very strong light. A figure within the light spoke to me: 'Do you want to remain here?' I replied: 'No, I want to go back and see my family and friends.' The figure said: 'You may go back for a short time. I will come again for you.' So, I returned to the body.*

Some months and many conversations later, Michael Cowlin follows up the subject of the accident and its aftermath. The following are extracts of various conversations he had with Peter over the succeeding year and that cover a variety of topics.

22/8/87
Peter: *Hello Dad. We are together again.*
Michael Cowlin: *Tell me about your passing over, Pete. Did you experience the out of the body and dark tunnel described by many people?*
Peter: *Not quite the same. I sort of came and stood by Mum and Fiona while they were rushing around with trolleys and then I found myself lifted up by those wonderful people who had been with me for several days and we drifted away over the hospital and Watford town. Then I found myself touching down on what seemed to be hard earth again over here. No dark tunnel, no river Styx. Just gently floating with others holding my arms through clouds, like when I used to do my flying! Yes, that's right Dad.*

23/8/87
Michael Cowlin: *You said the other night in the circle that you did not yet know why you had to go when you did, but that it*

seemed to have been pre-destined. Perhaps this will be clearer when you have moved through various stages and are more in contact with your higher self?

Peter: *Yes I think probably things are gradually becoming more clear, but there is much to learn.*

Michael Cowlin: *Pete, your mother feels that you must have departed when she left the bedside, but she had no feeling that you were standing with her and Fiona.*

Peter: *Well this all depends on your sensitivity and maybe she was overwhelmed by her emotions. That's all for now. Pete.*

9/9/87

Peter: *Dad, so at long last they have decided to hold the inquest! Well nothing new is likely to come from it. I shall be blamed for not stopping I suppose 'driving without due care and attention', which I suppose is true as I was half asleep and not fully concentrating. Lights have a hypnotic effect at night, and I think the colour of the car made it not show up until I was right on it. I should have stopped at the lights of course and I only have myself to blame for all the misery it has brought you two, Mum especially. I'm sorry and for Anne too. Hope she gets on well with Mark. She deserves someone nice to look after her. I will always be around for her, but sometimes I don't seem to be able to reach her. Tell her to think of me more when she feels sad or worried and I will come to her. And tell her to believe that we can communicate. That way it works better. Love from Pete the fanatic!*

11/9/87

Peter: *Dad, here I am again Pete the fanatic! So the inquest came to the conclusion that mine was accidental death. I think it was very much more directed than that! They tell me here that very little is the result of chance. Most chance things are either the result of karma, or the result of a plan of living, or the person's free will. I think I would have died about this time anyhow, from some cause if not the motorcycle. As you know I had a sort of feeling about this.*

8/11/87
Michael Cowlin: *Pete, you know about the inquest document that arrived?*
Peter: *Yes, I hope it didn't distress Mum and you too much. I do feel the responsibility of withdrawing from you, even though I had not expected it to go as it did. During the time I was unconscious at first I remember meeting a radiant person, like a light, who said, 'Go back', but I knew he only meant for a time. So don't blame the hospital staff too much. They couldn't have changed things. I realise that now. Please be happy for me, I hate sadness! Pete.*

17/7/88
Peter : *Only know I arrived here feeling a question of my departure should have been discussed.*
Michael Cowlin: *By whom Pete?*
Peter: *Me!*
Michael Cowlin: *You realised that you were going to depart from earth and we didn't? You felt on your side you should have indicated this? A bit of one thinks it would have been nice to know, but we may have been less relaxed.*
Peter: *I think from all angles it was right that way but I agreed before arriving here. I wanted to have time to say goodbye but at the time I could not find the time to tell you I knew.*
Michael Cowlin : *Did you have speech?*
Peter: *Yes.*
Michael Cowlin: *You started to speak a bit then you stopped. One wasn't sure it was a physical disability. Perhaps it was best, we might not have coped.*

164

Peter: I *prepared a speech for the occasion but it seemed inappropriate.*

Michael Cowlin: *What were you going to say?*

Peter: *I wanted you to know that I had planned the whole thing. I do not think you would have appreciated my motives at the time.*

Michael Cowlin *No, Pete. It is hard enough to appreciate them now!*

Peter : *I want you to know that I am always near when friends are visiting.*

Michael Cowlin: *It is still hard even now in spite of your close contact.*

Peter: *I feel it will be easier for you because our communications are so good.*

Michael Cowlin: *They are indeed, probably better than when you were on earth.*

Peter: *I arrived here a month late. I should have departed just after Christmas, but plans went wrong. I intended to have an accident when I went climbing.*

Michael Cowlin: *Yes, there was a question of you going climbing after Christmas. You would have been a long way off. Was this a conscious change on your part?*

Peter: *Yes, I realised you would not get to the hospital in time to see me alive.*

Michael Cowlin: *We would have tried, but a climbing accident might have been a sudden death. We were 24 hours late in reaching you due to stomach upsets. You were sent up to London and then back to Watford. We were later than we could have thought.*

Peter: *I realised you were coming. It must have seemed a long time to you, but I was outside my body and could observe what you were doing.*

Michael Cowlin: *You were aware of what we were doing at*

home here?
Peter: *Yes, got to go now.*

8/7/88

Michael Cowlin: *I am still intrigued, Pete as to whether or not you encountered this dark tunnel, or valley, at any stage in your departure to the other side. It has always seemed to me to be the means many people have of crossing the divide between Earth life and Spirit life, though some accounts seem to miss it out.*

Peter: *Well Dad, I certainly did not encounter a dark tunnel, or valley, during my death. When I came out of my body first of all, my encounter with the Being of Light was on or above the earth level.*

Michael Cowlin: *You mean he came down to this level, Pete?*

Peter: *Yes and the second time was when they came down to the hospital while I was in bed and stood around me. I knew it wasn't long then. When it finally happened and I was sick they lifted me so gently out of my body and we just rose through the hospital which sort of opened up and I went on till we touched down here. I had stayed long enough with Mum to watch them try to start my heart before we finally left for home here - no dark tunnel, or darkness of any sort - all light and brightness! I think the image of darkness is for those who haven't got much idea about life and death, which I am sorry to say, means most people in Western countries. Death to them is something awful, a dark oblivion, so perhaps the valley of the shadow of death is a sort of symbol to them and their passage through it dependent on having some spark of the Christ Power to keep them going. There are some that don' t make it and are lost in the darkness. We have to rescue them and this is the work that is suggested for the group, if you come together again - as I have a feeling you will.*

The extracts, taken from TRUTH IS VEILED, concern only the accident and events surrounding it. The book continues with information on a variety of topics including details of some of Peter's earlier lives and all manner of revelations substantiating the continuity of life.

And so death - where is thy sting? Where indeed? There is no sting. If one thinks of the four seasons - spring, summer; autumn and winter and of the continuity of life all around us, how can one imagine that human life suddenly becomes extinct at the point of so called *death?* It is a concept which makes no sense at all.

26

LETTING GO, LEARNING AND LIBERATING

I have learned more from my mistakes than from my successes.
Sir Humphrey Davy

Some men and women prefer to keep themselves wrapped up in the clothing of materialism and not admit to a spiritual life. They fear to do so because to acknowledge the spiritual side, which amounts to eternal life, will probably mean that they need to alter their values, moral standards and their whole attitude of mind.

There may be other reasons for rejecting the spiritual path. The materialist, young in soul, may thus far be unawakened to the inner light. Perhaps the individual, deep within, knows the situation but feels obliged to pursue a path on the outer plane. This may be because of a particular service he can render. Certain qualities of the character may be more prominent. For example the businessman may have a service to give to the commercial world and he will need highly tuned commercial instincts to succeed. It might be too much of a distraction to be aware of the light within - so it is mercifully veiled for the time being. As always we cannot judge the motive behind others actions.

Under certain planetary influences we will be required to relinquish certain things on the outer plane that we might like or to which we feel attached. But bear in mind that the Creator never takes without giving and what we might lose in one sense we gain in another. Thus we should welcome the testing philosophically, peacefully and even with joy. At this point the wise soul will know what has been lost will have served its purpose and something better awaits. Out of the ashes of the past something new is created.

Pain and suffering result when a soul clings to a condition that needs to be withdrawn. It is clearly difficult, for example, to let go of human relationships or material circumstances. Both are necessary and serve a divine purpose. We are experiencing through human emotion but we must not be enslaved by the personality, personal relationships, possessions, position or desire for these earthly things.

Renunciation does not mean withdrawing from the world but being free within. We are free when deep within the heart there remains a desire for nothing but to know more of the great white light and our wish is to become reunited with it. Renunciation is putting the outer material and personal things of life in the right perspective. It is possible to live in the world but not be of the world. We need to strive for a quality of meekness but not weakness.

At the moment most people think with the mind of the head. In future it is the mind of the heart which will come to the fore. We see it in those men and women who respond to intuition *(inner-tuition)*. When we are perplexed it is better to learn to be still and let the heart speak The direction we need will come to us in the form of a feeling or intuition. As our heart centres begin to open and develop we will recognise the true guidance of the mind of the heart and respond to it. If we listen to our heart centre, our true self - which believes with child-like faith and simplicity, in truth, goodness and light then all will be well. Unhappily, that earthly part of us is likely to intervene and pull us down. Thus we all too easily ignore the feelings of our heart centre.

Sentiment is often confused with love. It has its place but sentiment is not love. It can blind us to doing the right thing for real service to our fellow men. In giving foolishly we indulge not only our brother but, indirectly, ourselves. The devoted mother giving her child everything it demands imagines this is love. In fact, the mother robs the child of every chance of self expression and development by taking away opportunities for it to be happy and to grow. To withhold lavish expenditure does not mean she is cold and indifferent but rather that her love is of an order which allows her to see clearly the child's need for experience.

The best we can do for our companion is to be loving, understanding and sympathetic. Sympathise with his aims and aspirations but allow him free-will to decide on his own course of action. True love begets wisdom - in fact wisdom and love cannot be separated. To put the needs of our fellow traveller before our own and to see clearly his greatest need is true love. We ought never to be too busy to listen to a colleague in need and to help him practically, if that is necessary. When we are busy the temptation may be to put aside the needs of another but to show true love we have to let the other things wait and realise that his troubles are as real as our own. Some kind, gentle, constructive advice may be the turning point in his life. However, we must be guided by wisdom and not overwhelmed by sentiment in allowing that person to waste our time.

Pride of possession is a subtle temptation. We usually like to cling to possessions in one form or another. However, in due course, we need to arrive at that point of spiritual growth where we know that all possessions, gifts and attainments belong to God. Of ourselves we are nothing. We live and move and have our being only in the consciousness of our Father/Mother God. Once this is realised man is wealthy beyond all earthly dreams. When true wealth is understood man consciously becomes part of the great universal power, available for him to use not for himself but for the good of the whole.

Forced growth along the path of development is fraught with danger and if following such a path, great care is needed. The flower produced by unnatural growth can be delicate and prone to wither unlike its counterpart, which has weathered the storm, wind and rain and is likely to produce strong, fragrant flowers. Likewise the impatient soul forcing his development by speedier, but less thorough, methods may not weather future storms because his spiritual growth is not entirely sound or thoroughly tested.

The goal of man's spiritual quest is the realisation of God-consciousness which is achieved by surrendering the self. Man can hold nothing to himself because it goes against divine law. Giving himself truly he becomes at one with God, the universal life force. The *chakras* or *windows of the soul* open naturally and gently when we begin to live in a compassionate way - applying wisdom, love and service in our daily lives. Practising true brotherhood, for instance, stimulates the heart centre. As that develops the adjoining throat centre develops and radiates light. Then the brow centre stirs gently and opens to become an instrument of divine intelligence. The centres of the lower triangle *(solar plexus, sacral and base centres)* also begin to take more beautiful form, coming under the control and dominion of the higher triangle *(heart, throat and brow centres)* of wisdom, love and power from the Christ-man.

By truly serving our fellow men our own character and innate divinity will develop of its own accord. We need not worry about our spiritual growth - it will follow automatically. Once we begin to recognise and acknowledge spiritual laws we will find ourselves following a route of development that seems to have been prepared for us. We simply *let go and let God.*

27

MEDITATION AND REACHING UPWARDS

Our life is what our thoughts make it.
Marcus Aurelius

In the way that we travel to foreign parts in order to broaden our experience or to render service in some way our trip to earth, or incarnation, in a physical body is but an educational visit. We are only partially here on earth. We think we are here because we confuse our physical bodies with our true selves. That part of us here on earth is only an infinitesimal part of our whole being. When we incarnate, or visit, to take on a heavy physical *overcoat* it is hard to imagine that this is not our whole being.

We do not have to wait for our demise in order to contact the *heaven world.* Many people do it whilst they sleep and are aware of experiencing a real and vivid dream which leaves a deep impression afterwards - a vision, in fact. Such dreams usually come in the early morning, on waking. There are many types of dream and for many of us they are probably too confused and muddled to be of value and often they are likely to have been caused by bodily discomfort or over indulgence of some kind!

It is possible to prepare for the better type of dream and at the same time develop one's spiritual faculties. However this not something to be done lightly. One has first to aspire to do so from the heart and then, mentally, reach upward to the higher realms. It seems that we on earth need to make the effort, of reaching halfway as it were, if we really wish to commune with spirit. As we have been advised earlier, the door handle is on this side.

Meditation is the key. It has enormous value. The word has begun to mean a lot of different things but, in essence, it is contact with the eternal source of light and truth. By putting aside a few minutes night and morning we can help our body in self-control, train our mind and help bring body, mind and emotion under the directing power of the spirit.

The Creator has given us the power to realise and contact our higher-self. In meditation we can rise to higher planes and find ourselves in a world of light. This is where we find our celestial embodiment. Our celestial body is where we store the sum total of all the wisdom and good attained through many incarnations. It is linked with our limited personality of the earth via the bright flame of the Christ spirit in our hearts. Through meditation, by withdrawing into the stillness, we can link with the soul wisdom we have gathered through the ages and bring this wisdom into operation in our daily lives.

Anybody wishing to make a conscious contact with the spirit realms is advised to go about it in a gentle way. Everything should be done harmoniously. Within us is a power or divine will and this can be the motivating force which lifts us into the divine realms. According to our soul's awareness it will be taken to the place in the spirit world where it will find both lesson and refreshment and where it will meet up with old acquaintances. Such visions can serve to teach us and stimulate our spirit, reviving memories of the *ancient wisdom* which will assist us in our future work. What has happened in our soul's past moulds its future.

There are many ways of meditating but the essence of it is to find the place of absolute stillness and silence within. Thus it is helpful to sit motionless and to do this one must be comfortable. The spine is best held erect as if suspended from some imaginary thread which can be visualised as linking the meditator with the sun above. Gentle, rhythmic breathing will help us to detach from the earthly self. The natural thing is for the mind to wander and, if it does, then it is important to constantly, but gently, bring it back to focus on the breath.

In the stillness as we seek union with God we become quiet and peaceful. We become, even if it is just for a moment, a created being of light without judgement, fear or worry. We become peacefully wise. For an instant we ascend and touch on our true identity which is love. In meditation, we let all the rest fall away and breathe in and out this love and peace.

For some people this at-one-ness with all creation can be achieved quite differently. Gardening can be a meditation for some. Writing poetry, listening to music, watching a sunset or simply walking in a beautiful place will make the connection for others. For very busy people, who find it difficult to set aside a specific time in the day to be quiet, it is an idea to cultivate a greater awareness of the ordinary things in the daily round. This can be most useful as a mental discipline. Dedicating the washing up, the domestic chores or other mundane tasks as a time of concentration or awareness of the greater world can be rewarding. To be fully there in mind and body. The ancient teachers remind us that the present moment is all there is - the past is history, the future a mystery so it is important to enjoy the moment, the NOW.

One method to facilitate meditation is known as the *Ascension Technique* * This is the revival of an ancient technique taught by Ishaya monks and especially helpful for those people who experience difficulty in quieting the conscious mind.

There is so much in life to enjoy and through which we can grow spiritually. Quieting the mind on a regular basis is very helpful but it is important not to set too high a standard for ourselves - go easy on the self-judgement. Do what you can when you can and, in between, find time to smell the roses. Most of us try too hard, expending so much energy thinking and planning what we feel we ought to be doing and missing out on the joy of the moment.

All the answers can be found in the divine mind but we are obliged to rise above our physical selves to contact that aspect of ourselves. I say above the physical, which is true in one sense, but I really mean *going within to higher levels of reality*, tuning in to a different vibration or frequency to that *inner spiritual part* or existence. It is the spirit or light within each of us that has to be developed and, put very simply, this process is our purpose on earth. *We visit this planet in order to develop our spiritual selves*, to brighten that light within, the Christ spirit in all men.

We are told the elder brethren have a lively sense of humour and love laughter. They encourage happiness and a zest for living but there is a moment to be still and that time is when we seek communion with higher worlds. Such co-operation is necessary because *the link is a very fine and delicate vibration which works through the etheric body.* The etheric body, being interlaced with our nervous system, means that noise or discord breaks the fine contact.

Thinking of heavenly things and the spiritual world causes some people to wonder if what they see in meditation, or in contemplation of beauty, is real or merely the result of imagination? Anything that one strongly imagines one begins to create in soul substance. When creating in our minds, or in our imagination, we are creating in actual form in the soul world. Imagination is the doorway, the key into the soul world. What one imagines to be there is there and enduring. So we need to understand that by our thought, or imagination, we have the power to create real form in the soul world and that form can be externalised in the physical world.

*The Society for Ascension has a UK office at: The Steps, Church Road, Burley, Oakham, Rutland LE15 7SU. Telephone 01572 722465 Fax 01572 724634 and in the USA at 272 Biodome Drive, Waynesville, NC 28786. Telephone 828 926-7853 Fax 828 926-5250

28

GROWING SPIRITUALLY

Love all. Serve all.
Sri Sathya Sai Baba

The soul passes from childhood into man or womanhood and later sees for the first time the light which is to guide it further along the path. Seeing the light, or awareness of the spiritual dimension, is a great moment but with it comes responsibility. Whereas before, the soul walked in ignorance and darkness, now it sees the path which lies before it. There is a consciousness of the path ahead and individual responsibility is inescapable. Work begins in earnest. To reject that responsibility, which is to turn one's back on the light, is to invite sorrow. To reject the light, once seen and understood, breaks divine law and will attract consequences.

The new soul consciously setting out on the path will encounter many trials, tests, sorrows and difficulties. It is a time of great confusion. Despite trying hard the questing soul comes up against all manner of human problems. Spiritual difficulties complicate the picture and there is a temptation to stop striving for spirituality and go back to living in the outer world. This is a very testing moment and trust is required. We never know from one hour to the next what great awakening will be ours. One moment we are in darkness and in the next we are illumined.

The lessons each soul needs to learn are common to all humanity although they may be presented to the individual in unique form. We all face the same problems but wrapped up differently. We cannot learn from our brother's experience and likewise he cannot learn from ours. Equally we cannot fully understand another's experience unless we have undergone it ourselves. Hence the difficulty of judging another! It is important to remember that we are all of God and that our fellow men need our love and goodwill.

The light shines through windows of a variety of shapes and colours but ultimately all colours are blended in the one great ray of white light. Our neighbours path and our own may be quite different but whatever our path it needs to be followed steadily. Every path is good according to the level of consciousness and the karma of the individual who follows it and according to the needs of the general plan for the spiritual evolution of humanity. Every soul's experience is unique. For this reason it is not a good idea to try to bring everyone we know onto the same path. Different paths suit different people. *No one path is the only right one.* Individual souls will follow a path based on experiences gained in previous incarnations.

For our spiritual side to be of value to us it has to become a way of life and not simply an intellectual knowledge of the theory. A knowledge of music does not make a musician any more than occult knowledge makes a master. It is salient to note that the illumined saints and masters of the past have usually been simple men and women, without any great claims about earthly knowledge.

Spiritual growth results from the soul absorbing and digesting spiritual truths and putting the simple spiritual laws into practice in daily life. The sincerity and purity of the inner life and its response to the finer vibrations from the more subtle worlds is all important. Some look for a complicated teaching. This is, to some extent, a natural consequence of following bodily instinct. Since the brain is part of the body it may need to be fed! But highly intellectual foods are somewhat indigestible so we had best beware! It is as well to assimilate and live simple truths instead. *Seeing the light and subsequent initiation comes from spiritual experience rather than intellectual knowledge.*

For most of us the way of love, or mystical way, is much safer than forced occult growth. However, the mystical path may have its difficulties and heartbreaks so there is a need to be dispassionate. As one becomes very sensitive the effects of the words and actions of our fellows may disturb us unduly. There is a danger of becoming too introspective - having had our heart, throat and head centres stimulated in some degree. There is a need for inner strength and poise. Dispassion is called for and we need to turn our thoughts outward towards the well-being of others and not dwell on our faults and failings.

It is helpful to realise that all men are both pupil and teacher - a pupil to one and a teacher to another. When we have learned to be dispassionate our light will shine and we will appear to the elder brethren as a steady and reliable instrument to be used for constructive work amongst men. Until we have developed a dispassionate and steadfast manner the elder brethren will not know our reaction in certain circumstances. It is only when we have been thoroughly tested by the vicissitudes of life that we can be trusted to do whatever work is entrusted to us.

By cultivating dispassion and quiet stillness we will hear the still small voice above the clamour of the world. Will we know if that call is genuine? I think so if it tells us to do something that our conscience knows to be good, loving, kind and wise. Otherwise we can disregard it. The soul learns through sorrow and joy alike. If we fail to learn a lesson in one incarnation then we will be confronted with it in another and possibly subsequent lives until the lesson is learnt. It is worth being aware of such lessons coming our way and being thankful for them. Learning the lessons facilitates our spiritual evolution and facilitates the return journey to our Father/Mother God.

Minor initiations are continually being experienced in human life but the major ones are definite spiritual experiences. We are fully conscious of such experiences although it may take us a while to take it all in. The great upheavals, changes and decisions which come in the course of a human life can be regarded as relatively minor although we might not think it at the time!

Major initiations are experienced by those who have turned towards the light and are making progress on the probationary path. This causes a stimulation of the upper triangle of the heart, throat and head centres. The lower triangle which consists of the solar plexus, sacral and base centres may be involved too. All the points of light in man gradually grow into life from the eternal universal sun (the spirit behind the physical sun rather than the golden orb we see in the sky) eventually to become a blazing sun-star, a Christ. From God we come and to God we return.

As we unfold spiritually there may be an awareness of three paths running parallel but also overlapping one another. The first concerns the preparation of the physical body. The second concerns the preparation and training of the soul and thirdly the training and discipline of the awakening spirit. Tests await us in all areas.

On the soul vibration the first and greatest test is that of dispassion. It is difficult to keep our cool at all times - when we feel hurt or are displeased by somebody or want to give way to depression. Fear and discrimination are other tests. We need to discriminate between good and evil and understand what they are.

How often do we come up against some awful experience that we would do almost anything to avoid? We simply have to grin and bear it knowing that we are gaining wisdom in our heart and paving the way for further growth whilst paying off a past debt. It is a further opportunity to demonstrate dispassion.

Another trap for the unwary is that of spiritual arrogance. When we begin to make progress on the spiritual path we may think what wonderful people we are and begin to believe those who tell us such things. Standby for a test about spiritual humility! We need to remember that anything good that flows through us is that of the Christ life - of God. Without that we are nothing.

Treading the path to initiation is not always comfortable. We may wonder why our guide does not save us a lot of experience by prompting us to take the easy route. We have to prepare ourselves to go through dark places as well as sunlit ones. It is easier to go round a pond instead of falling into it but, if getting a ducking teaches us to swim, it has its value. Rather than looking upon such events as obstacles it is better to consider them as opportunities. Good and evil are alike as teachers.

As the soul grows it strives to shake free - to seek its freedom. It is not unlike a child growing up and struggling for self-expression and self-will. In doing so the child may scream and shout. The parent may well tolerate only so much of this behaviour before demonstrating his or her power. The struggle against authority gradually dies down and the child becomes docile whilst experiencing the love and strength of its parents. In the same way the fledgling soul eventually comes to know and trust the love and wisdom of its Creator. Rebellion is no longer necessary because it knows that the Parent-of-All is in charge and that the divine plan is perfect.

Imagine the Christ-like form of a young soul living in the higher realms but then *breathed forth* by the Creator in quest of spiritual evolution. The descent would be first through the higher spheres of life and then all the way down into densest matter. At first this fledgling soul is very much of the heaven world but from the first contact with life on the physical plane it begins to weave its soul garment. The ready receptivity of influence from the higher realms gradually fades as the effect of the denser world becomes more pronounced. The spirit within becomes more enclosed and the senses dulled so that communication with the higher worlds is attenuated. Thus man is imprisoned, bound and blindfolded, by the physical world in which he finds himself and where he may well remain for many incarnations. To those who are unable to understand it must be awful. It would appear that the soul is bound to the wheel of rebirth, has no freedom or opportunity to loosen his bonds and move forward.

However, on the higher planes, the development of the light within the struggling soul is observed. The light, at first masked and dimmed, gradually grows brighter. The journey of the soul in numerous earthly experiences, through the ages, is seen from the higher realms. In each life more light is absorbed. Perhaps it is through human love, be it only in crude form, that light comes to a particular soul? Or maybe it is because of love bestowed on flowers or animals? Whatever the source love helps the inner light to become brighter. A constructive reaction in trying circumstances can also cause that light to brighten.

Thus man journeys onward. The death of the physical body is followed, in due course, by rebirth in another body. There is a continuation of the cycle of soul journeys, but only after a period of refreshment in the higher worlds. It can be compared to a man walking a trying, weary route and growing tired by the evening. Eventually lying down to rest, the sleep refreshes him and he awakes in the morning as a man new-born, restored and renewed.

29

LOVE ONE ANOTHER

*The key to the kingdom of light, the kingdom of happiness, the key
to all progress is in your heart - it is love. Love one another and
be loved. Love begets love.*
White Eagle

Human life is dominated by the physical and material. Another
aspect lies buried deep in our subconscious until it is developed
and brought out into the conscious mind. This hidden aspect is
the spiritual one - the life of that higher part of our being.

For most of us material life has the greater claim on our
attention. In a sense this is as it should be, because it is only
through the physical life that the soul gathers the experiences it
needs to return towards God. But material life on its own is not
enough. Every aspect of our being has to be recognised, attuned
and perfectly balanced. Our aspiration towards spirit is of the
highest importance.

It is no use thinking that man's spiritual life can wait. The
progress and happiness of mankind depends on man's under-

standing of this attunement and *the balance between matter and spirit*. Until the human soul on this earth learns to recognise the spiritual aspect of life as the supreme light and purpose of it's being it will have the greatest difficulty in finding lasting happiness.

We might well wonder what purpose life serves. We are told *it is an ever-unfolding revelation of the beauty of God and of the meaning of love, wisdom and joy*. But what about sickness, suffering and sorrow? Of what use is all this talk of eternity to mortals who suffer and exist only by the sweat on their brow? What can it mean to the average man? I think we need to understand that trials and suffering are necessary to lead us to inner understanding. Only when we are able to realise this can we, then, experience overwhelming love and joyfulness. Suffering, it would seem, is the means of forcing the growth of the seed.

Before *letting us loose* in the world the Divine Mind conceived us, not as we are now or as we were ages ago but, as we will become in the fullness of time when we have been caressed by the Light. When we have grown from the soil and turned our faces away from the shadows and into the sunlight. We tend to think only of our present incarnation and for some of us *three score years and ten* is reckoned to be a fair innings. But it does not end there - that's only the start of it! Life is not just for seventy years but for eternity and it is continually unfolding.

In the meantime we may well be fearful or, at least, at some time or another in our lives we have been afraid. Fear is man's greatest enemy. Perhaps we fear some ordeal such as an operation or a big change in our life? Maybe we fear changing conditions because we are entering the unknown? If we look back over our lives we will know that what we feared most never happened. How many times have we found ourselves facing an unavoidable ordeal but when it came to the crunch we have come through the experience unscathed?

All of us have our particular problems. Nobody on earth is completely without difficulty of some sort. What may seem to be a small problem to others is a huge one for the individual concerned. We need to give some thought to such difficulties which sometimes impinge on our daily lives in a serious way. It is necessary to understand that our elder brethren, dwelling in the world of spirit and the celestial realms, are not without knowledge of the difficulties of earthly life. They love us and want to help. After all, many of them were our companions in former lives and are aware of the relationship between themselves and us.

Many people fear death because they do not know the meaning of death. Those in spirit have passed through death many times - and so have you and I. But our memory is blocked because we are in the valley. If we had risen to the heights we would have a clearer vision and would know there is no death. Simply a change of conditions - just a different state of life. There is nothing to fear in death because we do not die.

We must not forget that a wonderful provision has been made for every human being by the wise and loving Parent-of-All. This provision is that there are periods in our lives when we leave our hard work on earth and withdraw from the physical into a heavenly state. Our physical body dies. Moving in to that world of beauty and harmony we are refreshed and strengthened. It is difficult for us here on earth to conceive the beauty that awaits us in what orthodoxy calls heaven. One way to think of it is to imagine what it is like to have a wonderful holiday and return to work feeling full of energy and ready to continue with our plan.

For many of us work is far from interesting. It is wearying and boring but we, alone, have the power to make it interesting. Indeed, we need to do so if we are to fulfil ourselves in any way. Whatever our chosen task or whatever work life has placed before us we need to accept it with thankfulness. When we are doing our work we should do it easily, happily and quietly. Let it be a joy, not a burden. If we relax in our minds, are happy, feel loving, then all things will work together for good. Remember the expression: *do your best and God will do the rest.* It is for us to make the most of whatever conditions we are in. We need to make the best of life, be thankful for it and keep our vision on a goal which is all good.

I said at the beginning that earth's humanity has always looked to the sun. Every race has left on record its worship of the sun. The ancients knew that the source of all life was the sun and even beyond the physical life they knew that the sun was a spiritual manifestation of the one universal principle from which all life came. That principle is love and love is light. Where there is love there is light and there is radiance. In fact, where there is *light* there is en*light*enment. Where there is no love there is darkness and heaviness.

Can men and women ever understand that God intends them to be happy? That God does not punish them but rather they inflict their own punishment on themselves? People bring forward arguments galore in order to deny this simple, eternal truth. We do not like to be told that we are our own enemy and that we bring troubles on ourselves.

The Nazarene told us how to live - *love one another*. One could be forgiven for wondering how it is possible to love certain people who seem so naturally antagonistic towards us or, to love others who have committed terrible crimes? Firstly, we need to find peace in our own hearts because this is the only way to establish peace, good will and brotherhood on earth. It is not a bad idea to look at our daily habits of thought, especially any antagonistic or critical thoughts. Spoken criticism can be very destructive. The one who would become a disciple must start on himself, or herself, with love in the heart.

On the subject of love, it is the seed of divine love which distinguishes man from the creatures of the animal kingdom and other kingdoms of nature. Man has the capacity within his own heart to love divinely and selflessly. It is true that animals too have a great and, in a sense, selfless affection for their masters and the human friends who are kind to them. However, it is man alone who has been given the gift, or the ability, to love in both a human and divine or heavenly manner. This love or light is the spirit of Christ within him.

Incidentally, this light, or love, must extend to all God's creatures. How can the human family expect things to go well when it is cruel to the animal kingdom? Tame animals have to depend upon men and women. They give us their faith and look to us for food, protection and companionship but pain is sometimes inflicted upon them thoughtlessly, selfishly and needlessly.

It is in our interest to become more aware of the life-force in the air we breathe, in the water, in the trees and even in the stones. We need to treat not only God's creatures but the very earth itself, kindly, with imagination and with respect. We ought to feel love, tenderness and compassion for all.

Looking back with regret is a waste of time. We have all done things we might have preferred not to have done but it is important to move forward. We need to behave honourably and let that inner voice guide us so that, in whatever circumstances we find ourselves, we are careful what we say and always speak truthfully.

Whilst the earth appears to be chaotic at the present time it is worth remembering that what might appear to be evil is actually a tester of the human spirit and can quicken the growth of the light within - that light which is love. As I have written earlier the greatest mistake we can make is to think of ourselves as separate from God or from the universe into which we have been born. We are not separate but part of the one whole.

We human beings have an unfortunate habit of complicating our lives unnecessarily. Love is the most profound secret of the universe. This secret is displayed openly as if it were valueless. It's seed lies within every soul, although many, many incarnations may need to pass before the majority of souls discover the light which lies within their own being. Love is supremely simple, absolutely fundamental, requires no training, is permanently transforming, increases more as it is given away. It is here for all who wish to have it. The supply is unlimited and it increases from age to age.

What stands between any of us and the full experience and expression of love? Nothing at all! Love is the most natural expression of everyone's life, the one fundamental constituent of everything, the innermost basis of every feeling of every being in created time. It is simpler to experience love for everyone than to experience any dark emotion, any feeling of hatred or fear.

Simply put into effect the words of the Master - *love one another*. These three words, if truly understood and lived, would resolve all our problems. The whole will be healed.